Lyrics by Sameer

Sameer Anjaan is one of the most renowned lyricist in the Indian film industry. He holds the Guinness World Records record for being the most prolific Bollywood lyricist, with over 640 films and 4,500 songs to his name. Born Shitala Pandey, he is the son of the acclaimed poet and lyricist Anjaan. Sameer has garnered multiple accolades, including three Filmfare Awards and the prestigious Shaheed Bhagat Singh Award. With a career spanning over three decades, he continues to shape the landscape of Indian cinema with his poetic expressions.

Shuja Ali, also known as Ali Saeed Rizvi, is an accomplished screenwriter and director with a rich portfolio in Indian cinema and international television. Known for directing films and TV shows like *Kuch Log* (2011), *Fear Files* (2012), *Baat Bann Gayi* (2013) and producing the acclaimed sports reality web-series *Kumite 1 Warrior Hunt* (2023), Shuja's influence spans across India and stretches to countries like Singapore, the UAE, Afghanistan and Canada, marking him as a prominent figure in the entertainment industry.

Lyrics by Sameer

Stories behind the Iconic Songs

SAMEER ANJAAN
AND SHUJA ALI

RUPA

Published by
Rupa Publications India Pvt. Ltd 2024
7/16, Ansari Road, Daryaganj
New Delhi 110002

Sales centres:
Bengaluru Chennai Hyderabad
Jaipur Kathmandu Kolkata
Mumbai Prayagraj

P-ISBN: 978-93-6156-393-5
E-ISBN: 978-93-6156-946-3

First impression 2024

10 9 8 7 6 5 4 3 2 1

Printed in India

Contents

Prelude

Dear reader, the story behind the inception of *Lyrics by Sameer* is exceptionally distinct, and I, Shuja Ali, am thrilled to share it with you. Before stepping into the film industry, I used to avidly consume the captivating tales of the making of iconic films like *Mughal-e-Azam*, *Sholay*, *Mother India*, and more, through film magazines, TV and radio programmes. These narratives ultimately played an important role in shaping my decision to venture into the magical film industry. The remarkable stories, ranging from legendary director K. Asif's casting of Dilip Kumar to Madhubala's distinctive immurement in a wall, or the collaborative efforts of Naushad and K. Asif in persuading the renowned classical singer Bade Ghulam Ali Khan to lend his voice for Tansen, or how Amjad Khan prepared himself to play the role of Gabbar Singh—these anecdotes fascinated me a lot.

Upon entering the film industry, I would routinely hear my seniors share experiences and anecdotes from their lives. After spending 8–10 years in the industry, I, too, accumulated a treasure trove of unique stories. I began sharing with my juniors the story of my encounters with luminaries such as Dilip Kumar, Ashok Kumar, A.K. Hangal, Lata Mangeshkar, Khayyam, V.K. Murthy, and they always listened with great interest. I realized the deep influence these stories hold and their impact on the hearts and minds of dedicated enthusiasts of Hindi cinema.

One day, while having some industry discussion with my

close friends at a café in Andheri West, I looked outside the window and noticed the legendary lyricist Sameer Anjaan heading towards his building at the end of the road. Without hesitation, I quickly excused myself and rushed towards him. On reaching him, I extended my hand and introduced myself as a modest member of the film community to which he belonged. He graciously acknowledged my enthusiasm with a bright smile. This marked my first encounter with Sameer ji.

Later, I also visited his home to record an interview with him, during which he shared the behind-the-scenes anecdotes of some of his hit songs. These stories deeply touched my heart, transforming me into an even bigger and a more devoted fan of his craft.

Some time had passed when I happened to come across a prominent literary agent. By then, I had already directed and written a couple of feature films and television shows. Given my extensive experience and strong ties with Bollywood, the agent suggested that I consider writing a book on the film industry. Initially, I didn't take the proposal seriously, but after reflecting on my numerous articles, essays and scripts, I realized that I could indeed transition into an author. As I sought an appropriate topic for my first book, I checked my industry contacts. That's when I saw Sameer ji's name in my phone book.

I thought it would be a fantastic idea to unveil the fascinating anecdotes behind the songs of Sameer Anjaan. After receiving a go-ahead from my agent, it was time to approach my subject to seek his support and approval. Sameer Anjaan, a Guinness World Records record-holder for writing most number of songs in the world, graciously gave me his blessings and agreed to co-write a book on the hit songs of Hindi cinema written by him.

This was a wonderful opportunity for me to chronicle

the incredible stories behind some of the most successful songs of the 1990s and 2000s penned by Sameer Anjaan and predominantly composed by the highly accomplished Nadeem–Shravan, the most successful music composer duo of that era. Although it posed a challenge initially, the process became enjoyable as I collaborated with Sameer ji, gathering insights and anecdotes from him and transforming those moments into chapters.

Lyrics by Sameer comprises 50 chapters dedicated to Sameer Anjaan's timeless compositions. However, the book transcends the limitations of being merely a collection of a discography of one individual. Renowned for seamlessly blending poetry and romantic sentiments, Sameer Anjaan has significantly impacted the music industry. By opening the backstage door to the creation of the super-hit songs, we hope that the book would provide the reader an understanding of the extent of the impact. The book thus becomes not only a personal vessel but also a vessel for immortalizing narratives of the entire industry.

With this book, life seems to have come full circle for me. I once enjoyed reading or hearing interesting and engaging stories about the making of films and film stars. As my journey in the industry progressed, I began sharing my own experiences with my juniors. Today, the journey has evolved, presenting me with the chance to inspire others through the written word. With storytelling at its core, the medium has shifted from verbal to written expression.

While Sameer Anjaan, the lyricist, offers insight into the emotions behind each lyrical masterpiece, I, through a filmmaker's lens, add visual and emotional depth. This historical archive sheds light on the transformative power of collaboration, illustrating the enduring impact of musical artistry across generations.

Lyrics by Sameer is a journey through time, celebrating artistic brilliance and the lasting impact of melodies etched into Bollywood enthusiasts' collective memory.

So, here we are—Sameer ji and myself—welcoming you, the reader, to the enchanting realm of Bollywood melodies, as we embark on a musical journey through the pages of *Lyrics by Sameer*. We invite you to feel and understand the heartbeat of an era through Sameer Anjaan's timeless songs and immerse yourself in the captivating tunes of the 1990s and 2000s, a period renowned for its mesmerizing musical compositions.

—Shuja Ali

1

'Mujhe Neend Na Aaye'

1990

Friends, I would like to begin by talking about one of my formative experiences as a lyricist, which was with the Aamir Khan starrer *Dil* (1990). Even though I had been writing lyrics for some time, by the time *Dil* was given to me, I had not experienced enough success to call myself a well-known songwriter. It was extremely difficult for new songwriters to find a place in the film industry when it used to be dominated by established lyricists like Anjaan, Anand Bakshi and Majrooh Sultanpuri. The challenge for me was not simply about finding success in films but also to be able to escape my father's shadow and not just be known as 'Anjaan's son'. People often resort to using the term 'nepotism' these days when they see an industry veteran's son or daughter trying to find their way. But this has happened before as well; and when the veteran's child has talent, it ultimately shines through. I believed in myself, so I didn't pay much attention to what other people were saying, instead concentrating on my work. I was sure that, one day, my success will be attributed to *my* talent and not my father's.

Qayamat Se Qayamat Tak was one of the biggest hits of the year 1988 and had everyone raving about two things—its new star Aamir Khan *and* its music. Majrooh Sahab had penned the songs and Anand–Milind had composed them. The trend in the industry at the time was that no one wanted to mess with a winning formula. So, it was very obvious that Aamir Khan's next feature was supposed to go ahead with the same team as that of *Qayamat Se Qayamat Tak*.

I had a great rapport with Anand–Milind and had even written a few songs for them. But as a relatively unknown songwriter, I had no chance to write anything for *Dil*, which was the next movie they were offered. Aamir Khan, as the hero of the film, had insisted that *Dil* must have Anand–Milind and Majrooh Sahab. Although director Indra Kumar had wanted to work with Nadeem–Shravan—and had even signed them on—he had to relent to Aamir's pressure, eventually dropping the duo.

Indra Kumar had asked Anand–Milind to have a joint music sitting with the legendary Majrooh Sahab for composing the songs. In response, the musical duo had insisted that the director listen to the songs they had in their stock, and if he didn't like them, they would work with whomever he wanted.

So, the first sitting for the film's music happened without Majrooh Sahab where we presented pre-composed songs to Indra Kumar with great excitement. After listening to the stock, he liked 'Mujhe Neend Na Aaye' and 'Khambe Jaisi Khadi Hai' the most out of the many compositions we had presented. But Indra Kumar was not sure how to go ahead with a new lyricist like me over an industry legend that was Majrooh Sahab without offending him. On top of which he had the mammoth task of convincing Aamir Khan to give this opportunity to me.

The sitting ended on the note that he had 'liked two songs, but the words of the songs are too clichéd and there is no newness in them'. I was left with the job of reworking the songs and bringing freshness in them. Indra ji had said that he would try to convince Aamir once I had reworked the songs, or else, they would proceed with Majrooh Sahab as planned.

At that time, I was filled with confidence, as someone had liked my songs; so I got to working on them immediately. After writing 15–20 mukhdas of the songs, I presented them to Anand–Milind. They rejected all of them straight away since the lines did not flow well with the music. I pleaded with them to talk to Indra ji once and convince him that the songs were great in their original form itself. It didn't sound like a good idea to them but on my insistence, they invited Indra ji to listen to the songs again.

Indra ji had been under the impression that the new rewritten lyrics would be presented to him at the sitting. But when he came to know that it was the same song without any changes, he got upset. He felt that I was reluctant to taking feedback and rewriting the songs. Anand–Milind intervened and made him understand that the original words were best suited on the available tune and that they were confident of it being the best version of the song. Thankfully, Indra ji understood and told us to record the song, after which the final decision would have to be made by the lead actor of the film, Aamir Khan.

Udit Narayan and Anuradha Paudwal rendered their beautiful voices and made the song mesmerizing. After its recording, we all loved the song and the crew was utterly impressed by it. Indra ji was so convinced about its success that he said that he wasn't going to listen to anyone else's opinion of it. I was happy that after so much of struggle, the first song of the film could finally find its place. Indra ji went ahead to shoot a beautiful and romantic song sequence with Aamir Khan and Madhuri Dixit, both of who looked graceful and amazing on the screen.

'Mujhe Neend Na Aaye' became the most successful song from the film and one of the chartbusters of the year. I remember wherever we went for the screening of the film, we would witness people standing on their chairs in cinema halls and dancing the moment the song started playing.

Later, Indra ji came to me and apologized for all the heated discussions we had had during the making of this song. 'From now on I'll not argue with you on choosing words. You're their master,' he said in an apologetic manner.

'Indra ji, I was never rigid, but I was very confident about what I had written,' I humbly replied to him. We laughed at the friction we had had earlier and buried the hatchet.

After writing so many songs and having experienced so much in the industry, I can say that, most of the time, the first draft is the best. In search of perfection, you can wade through a thesaurus and make your words seem sophisticated, but the first instinct is usually right.

Movie: *Dil* | Lyrics: Sameer | Singers: Udit Narayan, Anuradha Paudwal | Music: Anand–Milind

∽

2

'Main Duniya Bhula Doonga'

1990

A*ashiqui* (1990) was a movie which was born out of its super hit songs.

During the recording of the movie *Baap Numbri Beta Dus Numbri* (1990), playback singer Anuradha Paudwal was impressed with Nadeem–Shravan and me, and she asked us to meet Gulshan Kumar, the founder of Super Cassettes Industries Limited, a very famous music label, which later came to be known as T-Series, to present our songs to him. Gulshan ji was a big name at the time, and we all were waiting for such an opportunity to come our way.

We went to meet Gulshan ji; he heard us patiently and appreciated our work. After the music sitting, he said that he wasn't working on any film projects at the moment. We were disappointed with the news, but it was as if Gulshan ji read our faces. He smiled and continued, 'You can give me all your ghazals for my current project, which is a music bank.' His idea was to make a bank of songs and pitch it to directors and producers who could pick from these songs according to the situation and mood in their films. Gulshan ji assured us if he didn't get any takers for the songs, he would release it as a private album. Although we were not impressed by the idea of making songs without a story, character or situation-brief, we really wanted to work with him since he was a titan of the industry. So, without wasting any time, we started working on our songs for the song bank.

The three of us started working on the music and recorded the first song of the album, which went: '*Main duniya bhula doonga teri chahat mein*'. After my first film *Dil* (1990), I had decided that I would keep the title of the film in the tent-pole song to hammer the title more and more in the minds of the listeners. '*Chahat*' (love; desire) was the keyword of this song because we had decided to name our album *Chahat*. We presented this song to Gulshan ji; he liked it a lot and asked us to work on more songs for the album. His appreciation was our motivation, and we set to work on creating more songs.

One day, Mahesh Bhatt came to know about Gulshan ji's music project and, on request, Gulshan ji let him listen to some of the songs we had composed. Mahesh Bhatt jumped up in joy on hearing these and was hooked on the compositions. He said, 'At present, I don't have any story with me in which I can put these songs but keeping the compositions in mind I can definitely come up with a story.'

We all were very happy as one of country's biggest directors was impressed with our work! In an interesting turn of events, rather than us working on the music for a story, Mahesh Bhatt was instead working on a film based on our songs!

Mahesh Bhatt wrote a romantic story and named it *Aashiqui*. One day, he called and told me that he would be using 'Main Duniya Bhula Doonga', but he had changed the title of the film from *Chahat* to *Aashiqui*. He then asked me to write a song with '*aashiqui*' as the keyword for the title track of the film. I wrote a song which went '*Sanson ki zaroorat ho jaise zindagi ke liye, bas ek sanam chahiye aashiqui ke liye*,' and presented it to him. Mahesh ji was very happy with the song and it was approved almost instantaneously.

During the recordings and sessions, we could see that Mahesh ji was incredibly happy with the music. This kept us motivated. The project was a very pleasant experience for us. One day during the recording, Mahesh ji teared up on hearing our song 'Tu Meri Zindagi Hai'. As soon as he heard the line '*Har zakhm dil ka tujhe dil se dua deta hai*,' he quickly took out his wallet and gave me all the money he had in it. He said that he had never heard such an expression. All the songs were ready and the entire album sounded so good that I knew it had to be a hit. We all began to eagerly await the release. But destiny had other plans for the three of us…

One day, Gulshan ji called me to drop a bomb. He said that he will not be releasing the songs of *Aashiqui* since he felt that it sounded more like a ghazal album rather than film music. He said, 'I don't want to make a film and waste my money on music which I don't have confidence in. I'll release it as a private album titled *Chahat* and our leading song will be "Main Duniya Bhula Doonga".'

I was disturbed by his call, to say the least, and rushed to inform Nadeem–Shravan about Gulshan ji's decision. Both the music directors were very disheartened and said that if this film doesn't see the light of the day then they would be finished, as they had put in a lot of time and resources into it. We went to meet Mahesh ji to discuss the matter further. He too was bewildered about how Gulshan ji could shelve the project just like that. We decided to see Gulshan ji in person and convince him somehow.

In search of Gulshan ji, we reached Sudeep Studio in Khar, where he was recording an album. Mahesh ji entered the studio shouting, '*Gulshan Kumar pagal ho gaya hai* (Gulshan Kumar has gone mad).'

Gulshan ji came out of the recording booth upon hearing such an insult. Mahesh ji confronted him about not releasing the music for *Aashiqui*. Gulshan ji told him that he was not confident that this kind of music would do well, and that after the super hit music of *Dil*, he wanted to keep the winning streak going. In response, Mahesh ji declared, 'From my experience, I think music of *Aashiqui* will be an even bigger hit than *Dil*.'

As we watched nervously, Mahesh ji grabbed a piece of paper, reached into his pocket for a pen and signed a blank paper stating that if the music of *Aashiqui* wasn't a hit, he would quit the industry and *Aashiqui* would be his last film.

Gulshan Kumar was moved by Mahesh Bhatt's confidence but responded with more concerns. He said that even if the music of the film performed well, he wasn't sure that the movie would do good business since the lead actors did not look like typical stars. Mahesh Bhatt assuaged his concern by saying that he could resolve this hitch by making a poster in which he would not disclose the lead pair initially. Although he was confident about both the music and the actors, he did this to reassure Gulshan ji. Seeing Mahesh ji confidence in *Aashiqui*, Gulshan ji promised to release the music and promote it to the best of his abilities.

That's how the iconic poster came to be! Mahesh Bhatt designed the poster of the film in which he showed a couple standing covered by a coat. Visionary Gulshan Kumar could now see the future of the film. To reach out to people and promoters, he got the poster of *Aashiqui* printed on packets of bangles, sarees, dresses, umbrellas, toys, bed sheets, etc. This branding worked in favour of the film. The success of *Aashiqui* and its music was a historical achievement. It sold several copies and made a lot of money for everyone involved.

I too earned my first Filmfare award for the song 'Nazar Ke Saamne'. The award will always be special to me because it was presented to me by my father, the legendary lyricist,

Anjaan. That is how the journey of a movie started with 'Main Duniya Bhula Doonga' and ended on an emotional, happy and successful note, the black lady in my hand.

Movie: *Aashiqui* | Lyrics: Sameer | Singers: Kumar Sanu, Anuradha Paudwal | Music: Nadeem-Shravan

3

'Tu Pyar Hai Kisi Aur Ka'

1991

After the phenomenal success of *Aashiqui* in 1990, film director Mahesh Bhatt and producer Gulshan Kumar teamed up once again to mesmerize audiences with their new offering *Dil Hai Ke Manta Nahi* (1991), starring Aamir Khan and Pooja Bhatt. Not only did this film turn out to be a blockbuster at the box office, but every single one of its songs became memorable. Let's talk about one of the most popular songs of this film, 'Tu Pyar Hai Kisi Aur Ka'.

Aashiqui's soundtrack was one of the major reasons behind its mammoth success. The magical team of Nadeem–Shravan and myself were the talk of the town, and we were getting offers to do every film left, right and centre. *Aashiqui* had made our life as enjoyable as easy with the amount of work we were doing.

The success that we had received through hard work and God's grace had given us many well-wishers and admirers, and at the same time had created rivals who were jealous of our work. I do not know who they were but some close friends of Gulshan Kumar had turned talebearers, poisoning his ear against us three. They would say things like, 'Success has ruined the minds of Nadeem–Shravan and Sameer, and they have forgotten the kindness of their mentor, Gulshan Kumar.

Too busy making professional relationships with others, they are turning away from him.'

However, these were mere lies being spread to malign us and our work and something that we were not aware of. When we came to know about this conspiracy against us, we tried to approach Gulshan ji but were unsuccessful. Soon we realized that he had already been swayed by these rumours. One day, we heard that he ji had said to someone, 'Nadeem–Shravan and Sameer are on cloud nine. I was the one who elevated them with huge success; who knows better than me the art of bringing them down? T-Series will give some of its songs to other music directors to teach them a befitting lesson.'

One of our songs, which had been recorded long ago, was cancelled by T-Series. This was a matter of concern for us and our careers. The three of us, as a result, gathered at Shravan's house to discuss this.

'Papa ji is avoiding us,' I told Nadeem. We used to address Gulshan Kumar lovingly as 'Papa ji'.

'Don't worry! Everything will be all right soon. I have a plan,' Nadeem reassured us.

On that particular day, I made a remarkable discovery about Nadeem—not only was he a musical genius with exceptional composition skills but he also possessed a unique talent for understanding the thoughts and emotions of others. A successful music director must also be adept at comprehending the producer's vision to maximize their creative potential. The legendary music director Kalyanji Bhai (of the Kalyanji–Anandji duo) once told me that if a producer comes and asks for a song, one's first job is to know where he is from. If he is from Gujarat, then you should first present him a garba style tune; if he has come from Uttar Pradesh, then you should make him listen to a 'Khaike Paan Banaras

Wala' type of a desi song, and if he is Punjabi, you must present to him a bhangra style song first. This will assure the producer that the music director understands him.

'Bhai, what's the plan?' asked Shravan.

'Look brothers, let us work according to my plan and I promise that if we will make him listen to a mukhda of a great song, Papa ji will record this song tomorrow itself. But let's make the song first.' Nadeem was confident in his plan and threw me a line for a song: *'Tu pyar hai kisi aur ka'.'*

I loved the line; it was so romantic.

'Pandit ji, let's develop this line further,' Nadeem asked me to take it forward.

'Brother, this line is very good, but where did the idea come from?' I asked Nadeem.

Nadeem looked at us mischievously and simply urged me to write. I repeated the line under my breath, 'Tu pyar hai kisi aur ka.' All of a sudden the next line rushed out of my mouth, *'Tujhe chahta koi aur hai'*. And thus this beautiful song of *Dil Hai Ki Manta Nahi* was born.

It was an amazing romantic song perfectly matching the situation of the film. The song was ready, but we were still facing the challenge of having to present this song to Gulshan ji in the first place.

We called Gulshan ji as soon as we were done with the song. 'Papa ji, no matter if you select this for a recording or not, you have to listen to this very powerful romantic song,' one of us said.

Gulshan Kumar had a great understanding of poetry and music and was always appreciative of good songs. Our enthusiasm must have been contagious, for he got excited and immediately called his office. But he added a caveat, 'Look, I do not have much time and have to go to a very important recording. I will only be able to spare a few minutes.' Gulshan ji disconnected the phone after this brief conversation.

We reached the T-Series office and, after a short wait, were called inside. As soon as Gulshan ji heard the song, we saw a smile erupt on his face. He had teared up. We realized that Nadeem's plan had been successful; Gulshan ji had the reaction we had expected. He embraced us and called his secretary to cancel all his meetings for the day.

'Get ready for an amazing song, we *have* to record this today itself.' Gulshan ji ordered his personal assistant. I looked over at Nadeem for an explanation, but he just winked at me.

All the bitterness had melted away in an instant. Later, Gulshan ji came to know that whatever he had been told about us was utter rubbish. Anuradha Paudwal and Kumar Sanu gave their stunning voices to 'Tu Pyar Hai Kisi Aur Ka', and *Dil Hai Ke Manta Nahi* proved to be a smash hit at the box office.

Movie: *Dil Hai Ke Manta Nahi* | Lyrics: Sameer | Singers: Kumar Sanu, Anuradha Paudwal | Music: Nadeem-Shravan

4

'Dekha Hai Pehli Baar'

1991

After the success of *Aashiqui* (1990), I was flooded with offers to write lyrics for almost every big film. One such film was *Saajan* (1991) in which I was supposed to work with legendary music director duo Laxmikant–Pyarelal. I was thrilled to work with both of them. After all, I had grown up listening to their songs and was a big fan. *Saajan* had an all-star cast with Sanjay Dutt, Salman Khan and Madhuri Dixit in it. It was produced by Sudhakar Bokade and directed by Lawrence D'Souza. I was happy and excited to write for *Saajan* because it was a film about a poet's life. Being a poet myself, it was going to be a new and interesting experience for me.

We started the music sittings and soon recorded a song which had a nice composition. One day, when I went to meet Laxmikant–Pyarelal ji at their office for a music session for the next song of the film, I was told to wait in the lounge. Sudhakar Bokade, the producer, also turned up for the music sitting. We were waiting for the scheduled meeting to start when we saw Subhash Ghai enter the office. Ignoring us, everyone got busy with Subhash Ghai who was the showman of Bollywood at that time. After sometime, Laxmikant–Pyarelal's manager came to inform us that our appointment had been cancelled because of Subhash ji's arrival and that we would soon be given a new appointment for the music sitting. Sudhakar Bokade naturally got very upset with the ill-treatment and took it personally. Considering it his insult, he decided to drop Laxmikant–Pyarelal from the film. Since he had been very impressed with my work in *Aashiqui*, he asked me if I could introduce him to Nadeem–Shravan. It was an era without cell phones. With a lot of difficulty, I somehow managed to reach Nadeem–Shravan. When I told them that Sudhakar Bokade wanted to meet them for his film, both got excited and asked me to come along with Sudhakar Bokade to their music room.

The encounter with Sudhakar Bokade was truly delightful, as he entrusted us to work on the songs. Nadeem–Shravan graciously invited him to listen to their compositions the following day. Sudhakar was thoroughly pleased with our work and expressed his gratitude to Subhash Ghai, acknowledging that the music for *Saajan* was now in capable hands.

We were ready with the songs in record time. Lawrence D'Souza and the cast of the film were very happy with the music. But I was still missing a song in the film which I could call its title song.

One day, as I was sitting in Shiv Sagar restaurant with Nadeem and Shravan discussing some other project, a line hit my mind. '*Dekha hai pehli baar, saajan ki aankhon main pyaar.*' I immediately recited it to the musical duo. Both Nadeem and Shravan were excited to hear it. Nadeem cleared the cutlery from the table and started drumming as if playing a tabla and asked Shravan to sing the lyrics. They composed the song then and there. I was finally satisfied to have a title song, but there was another problem. How do you place a song in a film that is almost complete?

Nadeem called Sudhakar Bokade and requested him to

somehow include the song. Even though Sudhakar liked this composition, he was not happy with the suggestion made by the music directors. After all, the film was almost finished and ready for release. On top of everything, the stars couldn't have been available to shoot. So he asked us to drop the song. Nadeem requested him to call Salman Khan and Madhuri Dixit, and make them listen to it once. He had a plan—if they liked it, then they would be able to give dates for shooting; if they didn't, we would drop it and not argue any further. Sudhakar Bokade agreed. He booked the studio for the very same evening for a music session with Salman and Madhuri.

Later in the evening, we presented the song to the two actors. Just as I had been hoping, they both loved the song. Salman declared that this song could not be left out of the film, insisting on going to Ooty the very next morning and shooting it. Travel tickets were booked, and the choreographer was asked to work on the dance overnight. Nadeem, Shravan and I worked the entire night to complete the song and gave the producer the finished version early next morning. The music video was shot within a day, which was an almost impossible task.

Saajan was a very well-made film. The movie would've done well at the box office even without this song, but the last-minute addition helped the film in a big way. It went on to become the chart-topping song of the year. During the film premiers in many cities, we witnessed the hold this song had on the public. The audience hummed along and danced to it in the theatres.

Nobody knew that this song had been lying somewhere in my subconscious for a long time. '*Saajan saajan pukaroon galiyon mein, kabhi phoolon main dhoondoon kabhi kaliyon mein*' was made more than two decades ago for another film titled *Sajan* (1969). The song was penned by my favourite lyricist

Anand Bakshi. This mesmerizing song of old *Sajan* had inspired me to write the title song of new *Saajan,* which has created a place for itself in the history of Indian cinema.

Movie: *Saajan* | Lyrics: Sameer | Singers: Alka Yagnik, S.P. Balasubrahmanyam | Music: Nadeem-Shravan

5

'Maine Pyar Tumhi Se Kiya Hai'

1991

The song 'Maine Pyar Tumhi Se Kiya Hai' appeared in the 1991 film *Phool Aur Kaante.* It was today's megastar Ajay Devgn's debut film, and he was being introduced as an action hero. Action was in Ajay Devgn's blood since his father was a legendary action choreographer and stunt coordinator.

In the '90s, Bollywood had a hit combination in music production and that was Nadeem–Shravan and Sameer. Every big filmmaker wanted to work with us but we were very careful in taking on new projects and often went through the script carefully before accepting to work on the film. One day, we were approached by actress Aruna Irani's husband Kuku Kohli who was directing a film. After the script narration, we loved the story idea and we could see that this film had a good scope when it came to background music and score. The best thing about Nadeem–Shravan was that they used to keep the hero of the film in mind while composing the song. That is why Nadeem asked the director about the lead cast of the film. Kuku told us that he was going to launch a new actor and actress and that both were really good.

We started working on the music and after few sessions I presented a mukhda of the first song to Nadeem–Shravan,

'*Maine pyar tumhi se kiya hai*', which they liked almost instantly. Kuku Kohli and the producer Dinesh B. Patel also liked the mukhda and we got the go-ahead from them. Before leaving, Kuku Kohli asked Nadeem if he could bring the hero of the film for the next music session. Nadeem smiled at the question and said, 'Yes, of course!' Nadeem–Shravan started putting their finishing touches to the song. Nadeem had decided to start the song with the sound of fingers snapping and clicking and said that this was a good luck click for the song and that this way the song would 'click' with the audiences. We were ready to present the final song to the producer and director.

Kuku Kohli entered the music room along with an average looking young boy who looked nervous. He introduced him to us as Ajay Devgn. Nadeem got upset and immediately left the room. I noticed and followed him out to find out his sudden displeasure. I saw he was pacing up and down in the corridor. I approached and asked him why he was so disturbed. He said that if this was the hero of the film, then he couldn't make the music and suggested that we should drop this film.

I requested Nadeem to calm down and called Kuku out of the room to discuss the matter. Nadeem was very straight forward with Kuku. He right away refused to do the music for the film—point blank. He looked at the director and said, 'Is he star material? It looks like you've picked him from the streets.'

Kuku requested him to stay for the film and assured Nadeem that the boy had potential in him to be a big star. Nadeem laughed at him for speaking up for Ajay. Finally, Nadeem agreed to do the music on the condition that the hero of the film would never come to our sessions because we need motivation to create magic and Kuku's hero 'who doesn't look like a hero' would definitely not do so, and Nadeem feared that the music would suffer as a result. Kuku agreed and accepted the condition. It was decided that we were not to have the hero for any music sessions.

We worked really hard on the music which turned out really well. Nadeem always used to say that the music would be a big hit but the film would flop because of the leading man. As expected, the music of *Phool Aur Kante* was super hit and 'Maine Pyar Tumhi Se Kiya Hai' was one of the most loved romantic songs of the year. Before the release of the film, Nadeem kept saying that we were duping the audience by presenting such a melodious song with a mismatching face. They would assume that good-looking actors were singing the song. But after seeing an unconventional hero on screen, they would start singing '*Maine hate tumhi se kiya hai*'. Kuku Kohli invited us for a trial show, but Nadeem refused to go just to avoid looking at Ajay Devgn.

During the premiere of the film at Gaiety Galaxy cinema in Bandra, as we were getting down from our cars, people started showering their love and affection by shouting our names, Nadeem–Shravan–Sameer, in one breath. I spotted the hero Ajay Devgn in a suit, standing with the rest of the cast and crew. He looked very down to earth. I went ahead to meet and congratulate the director Kuku Kohli, and Ajay. I thought Nadeem and Shravan would also follow me, but when I turned back to look for them, both Nadeem and Shravan had gone inside the theatre just to avoid meeting Ajay Devgn.

After watching the first 10 minutes of the film, I saw Nadeem rush out of the theatre. He was in search of Ajay. As soon as he spotted Ajay in a corner, he hugged him and congratulated him for his incredible debut. Nadeem confessed to Ajay that for the first time in his career he had misjudged someone. Nadeem told him the entire story from the very first sitting till the premiere; how much he had disliked him.

Ajay was such a sport; after listening to the entire story he laughed, hugged and thanked Nadeem for composing a brilliant soundtrack for his first film. That is how with a big hit like *Phool Aur Kante* our industry got introduced to the brilliance of Ajay Devgn.

Movie: *Phool Aur Kante* | Lyrics: Sameer |
Singers: Kumar Sanu, Anuradha Paudwal |
Music: Nadeem–Shravan

6

'Dhak Dhak Karne Laga'

1992

After the massive success of the movie *Dil* in 1990, producer Ashok Thakeria and director Indra Kumar produced and announced their second film in 1991 to be titled *Beta*. Except for the lead actors, they decided to repeat their entire old team, as it was a winning combination. The film featured Anil Kapoor, Madhuri Dixit and Aruna Irani in pivotal roles.

Since *Dil's* music had achieved big success, the second time around, Indra Kumar naturally had great expectations from Anand–Milind and me.

'Brothers, *Beta*'s music should be bigger than *Dil*'s,' Indra ji said to us.

But when the time came to present our songs to him, he rejected all the mukhdas we gave to him. It was very difficult to work with Indra Kumar because he did not like anything easily. The only way to work with him was to keep working hard, keep searching for new lyrics and music and keep presenting him with new renditions of our ideas. It was not possible to simply convince him by writing new lyrics and making fresh compositions. To satisfy him we had to find pre-recorded music from regional Indian cinema or world cinema as reference to get him to understand what the final result would sound or look like.

'Brothers, give me a song like "*Kate nahin kat te ye din yeh raat*",' he gave us a reference this time around.

'Kate Nahin Kat Te' was a very popular and sensual song from the film *Mr India* (1987). It was picturized on Sridevi whose dance and grace had elevated the video and had immortalized the song. After that, every producer–director wanted to have at least a song like 'Kate Nahin Kat Te' in his film which could ensure its success. Indra ji was no different pushing us for a song like that.

After that, Anand–Milind and I made an uncountable number of mukhdas and tunes. Indra ji used to hear them and reject them all. But we kept making songs in the hope that one day he may say 'yes'. Then one day both the producer and the director very happily came to the studio.

'We've got the song,' Indra ji said happily.

I understood that he has heard and liked an already composed song from some other music director for his film.

'Congratulations! If you've got the song of your choice, so why do you need us now?' Anand asked him.

'No man, it's not like that. Wait, I'll explain,' Indra ji gestured to us to sit.

It was the era of the VCR. Indra ji quickly loaded a VHS cassette into the VCR and switched on the TV. A South Indian song started playing on the TV set. It was a Tamil song 'Abbanee Tiyyani', filmed on Sridevi and Chiranjeevi, which was composed by Southern music maestro Ilaiyaraaja.

'Guys, copy the tune!' Indra ji proudly said to us.

Like I said earlier that Indra ji only understood 'a ready-made product' and that's why he was impressed by a superhit song and asked us to copy it. But it was not easy to make a hit Hindi song on a Tamil tune.

We had no issue because the film *Beta* itself was also

not an original film but an official Hindi remake of a Tamil superhit film, *Enga Chinna Rasa* (1987).

Anand–Milind's task had become considerably simpler as they stumbled upon a pre-composed tune and groove that provided a solid foundation for their work. However, the true challenge lay before me. I faced a blank slate when it came to writing lyrics for the distinct '*tat tat ta tat tat ta tara*' sound. I had to consider multiple aspects, including ensuring the ending of the sound synchronized seamlessly with the new lyrics, while also meeting the director's request for a touch of sensuality in the song.

> After hearing the tune again and again , a few words came to my mind: '*Dhak dhak karne laga, jiyara darne laga*'.

It fitted the tune perfectly. Anand–Milind jumped up on hearing the mukhda. Indra too liked it very much. I completed the lyrics by giving it the feel of a folk song.

Anand-Milind, with their hard work and creativity, took this song to another level. Everyone was very happy with the end result. Since the music of the film was going to be released by T-Series, the song was to be sung by Anuradha Paudwal. While recording at Sudeep Studio, she added the word 'ouch' to the lyrics from her side and made the song sensual right from the beginning. I remember that Udit Narayan had shared a joke with Anuradha ji, which made her angry and for a while the studio atmosphere was quite tense, but on the mic Udit Narayan supported her by singing the male part of the song by matching her mastery. Choreographer Saroj Khan was available at the recording and, with her eyes closed, was busy planning the shots and dance moves.

'Now you guys just see what *dhamaal* I'm going to do

with this song,' Saroj Khan predicted the fate of the song to us before leaving the studio.

And she proved herself right by choreographing it brilliantly and turning it into an everlasting dance number. Madhuri followed the dance instructions of her 'Master ji', the great Saroj Khan, to the T. On release, when people saw the magic of Madhuri dancing on the big screen, they were hypnotized.

Anuradha Paudwal and Saroj Khan won awards for immortalizing the song. Anuradha ji won the Filmfare award for the best playback singer while Saroj Khan won the Filmfare award for best choreography. Anand–Milind were nominated for the best music director but lost to Nadeem–Sharavan for *Deewana* (1992). But Anand–Milind received a bigger award later when they were praised by Ilaiyaraaja himself, who was the creator of the original tune of this inspired song. I wasn't nominated for 'Dhak Dhak Karne Laga', but that year turned out to be very lucky for me because I received my second Filmfare for *Deewana*'s 'Teri Umeed Tera Intezaar'.

The success of this film turned Madhuri Dixit into a superstar, and the success of this song gave her a new identity—she began to be called the 'Dhak Dhak Girl'.

Movie: *Beta* | Lyrics: Sameer |
Singers: Anuradha Paudwal, Udit Narayan |
Music: Anand-Milind

7

'Teri Umeed Tera Intezar'

1992

The film that marked the debut of two lead actors, Shah Rukh Khan and Divya Bharti, along with megastar Rishi Kapoor, was *Deewana* (1992). It was produced by Guddu Dhanoa and directed by debutant director Raj Kanwar. Shah Rukh had already started shooting for Hema Malini's directorial film *Dil Aashna Hai* (1992) much before this, but since *Deewana* was released first, it is considered to be his debut film. *Deewana* was an amazing name for a film and had a wonderful story. Nadeem–Shravan were once again entrusted with a film on their favourite subject, a love triangle. This film had a scope for great music! And that is what we did; the three of us began composing songs with complete vigor.

When a film project is announced, its fate can never be predicted. But not for *Deewana*. Perhaps, Nadeem knew that *Deewana* was going to be a memorable film, as one day around the completion of the album, when I reached Nadeem–Shravan's studio, I saw a tailor taking their measurements.

'Preparing to go to some wedding, brothers?' I laughed and asked them.

Nadeem asked the tailor to take my measurements as well and indicated to me to keep quiet. Well, since it was their studio I was in, I couldn't say no and allowed the tailor to take my measurements too.

'What was this for, Bhaijaan?' I asked Nadeem after the tailor left the studio.

Nadeem replied confidently, 'Making suits for the Filmfare Awards. The three of us are going to get a Filmfare for *Deewana*.'

'Well, actually, shouldn't I be the one doing the predicting, since I'm the pandit here?' I laughed seeing their overconfidence.

'My prediction is not given on what will happen tomorrow but by looking at what is happening today. Pandit, we are making excellent songs and inshallah we will get great rewards,' Nadeem said to me with excitement.

Every artist wants his creation to be loved and appreciated, so I also wished for what Nadeem had just said and got busy with work. Unforgettable songs like 'Aisi Deewangi', 'Sochenge Tumhe Pyar' and 'Payaliya' had been composed by them.

A new boy who was cast as the second lead in *Deewana* would often come to the recordings and watch us work for hours and hours. At that time, we did not know that he was going to be the superstar of tomorrow. But seeing his passion and interest in music, we often used to discuss that this boy, Shah Rukh, has a bright future ahead.

'Sir, you guys are making all the good songs for Rishi Bhaiya only. Please give me a good song too,' one day Shah Rukh said to us with quite hesitation.

On hearing this, the three of us looked at each other and for a while there was silence in the music room. Shah Rukh looked afraid. He feared he had offended us. However, the next moment, Nadeem's laughter ended the silence.

'Okay my brother, we will do something just for you,' Nadeem said to Shah Rukh.

He was very happy to hear this and lit a cigarette and took

a deep puff of relief. Soon after he left the music room, we started making a song for him that went '*Koi na koi chahiye pyar karne wala*'. With Shah Rukh riding a bike while singing this tune, the song was superbly shot by Raj Kanwar.

The young man who started his silver screen career with the song 'Koi Na Koi Chahiye' was probably unaware of the fact that he was going to be loved by the entire world as Shah Rukh Khan, the Badshah of Bollywood.

We had decided among ourselves that, for all the song in the film, I would write the lyrics first and then both the music directors would compose the tune. Barring one. This strategy was reversed for 'Teri Umeed Tera Intezaar'. For this track, Nadeem-Shravan composed the track first and then asked me to write the lyrics. It was a melodious composition. Finally, 24 hours later came the day when I was supposed to narrate the lyrics that I'd completed.

'Brothers listen to what I wrote on the tune you gave me yesterday,' I was excited to narrate my poetry to them:

Teri umeed tera intezar karte hain
Aye sanam hum to sirf tum se pyar karte hain

Both were very happy to hear the mukhda I'd written, with Nadeem saying, 'Pandit, this is simply brilliant. Especially, your use of the word "sirf". It underlines the character of a sincere lover. Wow!' Nadeem complimented me.

After that, both of them finished the song and presented it to the producer, director and actors. All the songs of this film had come out very well but the song 'Teri Umeed Tera Intezar' was received with an even more open heart and greater words. Rishi Kapoor hugged me affectionately and thanked me for writing such a remarkable song for him.

Sadhana Sargam and Kumar Sanu were called to sing the song. They gave it a new high with their melodious voices.

Raj Kanwar shot it brilliantly with Rishi Kapoor and Divya Bharti. They looked amazing on screen and the song received rave reviews.

Upon release, *Deewana* went on to become the second highest-grossing film on the box office in 1992. Critics wrote great articles, praising the film and especially the music.

Nadeem's prediction came true and I was nominated for best lyrics for 'Teri Umeed Tera Intezar'. Shah Rukh was nominated for the 'Best Debut Actor' award, and the sensational Divya Bharti received the nomination for the 'Best Debut Actress'. Nadeem–Shravan were nominated in the 'Best Music' category, and the 'Best Male Playback' nomination went to Kumar Sanu. *Deewana* won five awards at the 38th Filmfare Awards.

Majrooh Sultanpuri had been nominated for penning 'Woh Sikandar Hi Doston' from the film *Jo Jeeta Wohi Sikandar* (1992), while I was nominated for 'Teri Umeed Tera Intezar'. As soon as the anchor announced the nominations, the great Majrooh Sahab stood up and started walking towards the stage thinking that his name had been announced as the winner. But when the anchor declared the winner, 'And the award goes to Sameer for "Teri Umeed Tera Intezar",' Majrooh Sahab froze on the spot. But I ran up to him from behind and requested him to accompany me to the stage, saying that he was my guru and that I would only accept the award from my guru's hands. He patted me on my back with affection and walked with me to the stage to hand me the black lady that we in the film industry could die for in our careers.

Movie: *Deewana* | Lyrics: Sameer | Singers: Kumar Sanu, Sadhana Sargam | Music: Nadeem–Shravan

8

'Ghunghat Ki Aad Se Dilbar Ka'

1993

We do many things in our lives, but the work that is appreciated, respected and remembered by people becomes the most special. One film that was very special to me was *Hum Hain Rahi Pyar Ke* (1993) and its song 'Ghunghat Ki Aad Se Dilbar Ka' which got me the third Filmfare award of my life.

Today, Aamir Khan is globally regarded as an actor. But apart from acting, he is also admired as a producer and director. He has produced many landmark films, but his inclination has always been towards making films for or around or starring children, such as *Dangal*, *Secret Superstar* and *Taare Zameen Par*. All these films were commercially and critically successful. I would like to remind you of a film that he made long before these films, *Hum Hain Rahi Pyar Ke*. Although it was more of a family drama than an out-and-out children's film, it definitely must have inspired Aamir to take the baton forward to show children as protagonists in many of his films in the future.

Mahesh Bhatt was chosen to direct the film, Nadeem–Shravan were picked as the music directors to compose the music and I was given the responsibility of writing the lyrics by film producer Tahir Hussain, Aamir's father. Aamir Khan and Juhi Chawla were playing the lead characters. Since this was his home production, Aamir was very active in the project. Aamir not only starred in the film but he also co-wrote the script and screenplay with Robin Bhatt.

The songs for the album were being composed as usual, but there was one song where we got stuck. We were very excited about the tune, but I wasn't able to quite come up with any lyrics for it, and when I did, they were rejected. Finally, I wrote an amazing mukhda after some time:

Ghunghat ki aad se dilbar ka deedar aadhura rehta hai,
Jab tak na pade aashiq ki nazar shringaar adhoora rehta hai.

To me, it was a very romantic thought. Full of enthusiasm, I went to narrate it to Nadeem–Shravan at their office. Both the musicians were very happy with the lines. Next, I wanted the film director Mahesh Bhatt to listen to it and get his approval as well. But Nadeem disagreed with me and said that they would compose the song first and then tell Bhatt Sahab about it. 'This is very powerful, Pandit ji. Don't worry, he will definitely like it,' he had said.

Both musicians got occupied in composing the music with full energy. A great track was ready, and just when I thought that Nadeem would now call Mahesh Sahab to take his approval, he said that a half-cooked dish should not be offered to anyone. Kumar Sanu and Alka Yagnik enhanced the music with their magical voices and made the song sound even more beautiful. According to Nadeem, the dish was now ready to be served.

'Bhaijan, we've made an award-winning song for your film. You can come and listen to it.' Nadeem called Mahesh Bhatt in excitement.

The issue with Mahesh Bhatt and his brother Mukesh Bhatt, who was also the producer of the film, was that they would never arrive anywhere together. As a result, there would always be delays. The same thing happened that day too. Mukesh Bhatt reached before Mahesh Bhatt. After waiting a little for his brother, Mukesh Bhatt said that since Mahesh Bhatt was probably going to be late, we should all go ahead and make him hear the song. Although all of us wanted the song to be heard in Mahesh ji's presence, we complied with Mukesh ji's insistence.

Nadeem–Ṣhravan, all the musicians and I were eager for the producers to love and accept our work, so we quickly started the session by playing the song. Mukesh Bhatt also looked excited and eager to hear our work. He was looking at the screen and we were looking at his face. Soon, the song was over and it was apparent from Mukesh Bhatt's face that something was not right.

'No... Music is good... But the lyrics won't work.' Mukesh Bhatt dropped a bomb on all of us.

'Why, what's wrong with the lyrics, Mukesh ji?' Nadeem asked confusedly.

'See, we're making a family film and the words '*aad se*' is sounding like a slur, which will definitely not work.' Mukesh Bhatt was sure about his comment.

We all were very surprised to hear his feedback, which was correct to an extent. We'd mistakenly used an unmusical word. But at the same time, the words '*aad se*' seemed to fit very well with the music. Nadeem was deep in thought and asked the engineer to play the song and heard it twice. Nadeem's facial expressions showed that he was satisfied with the song. He repeated that he did not find anything wrong, and if the words were tampered with, the song would be spoiled.

Mukesh Bhatt suggested we tried using synonyms of the objected word. We also fiddled around with phrases like '*ghunghat ke peeche se*', '*chilman ke neeche se*', etc., but none of them were working at all. Amidst all this, Nadeem finally seemed to lose his patience and said, 'Sir, if you do not like the song, then leave it, we'll make something else for you but let us not spoil this song.'

We all knew Nadeem to be a little blunt. With his comment, there was a sudden tension in the atmosphere. Mukesh Bhatt had not expected this response from Nadeem. He stood up and stormed out of the room. That's when we all heard the voice of Mahesh Bhatt. He, in his quintessential style, where he could inject warmth into any environment with his infectious energy, entered the room with a wide smile on his face, Mukesh Bhatt by his side.

'Nadeem, let me hear my award-winning song!' he announced to pep everyone up.

It took Mahesh Bhatt another second to read the room. He understood that there was something wrong after seeing everyone's faces. 'What happened, Nadeem?' Mahesh Bhatt asked with some concern.

'Mukesh ji did not like the song. He is saying that we've used an abusive word,' Nadeem grumbled.

'What! Let me hear the song first,' asked Mahesh Bhatt.

Mahesh Bhatt listened to the song twice on loop. As soon as it was finished, he looked at Mukesh Bhatt with anger.

'Your job is the production of the film. Don't try to be creative,' Mahesh Bhatt chastised his brother.

Having said this, he applauded the song by embracing Nadeem, Shravan and me, and promised to use the song as it is in the film. As soon as the songs were released, people were full of praise for it. Till date, no one has pointed out or criticized the oddity of that particular word. I think the audience does not pay attention to any single word or instrument or any other singular element in isolation in a song. They either like and accept the whole package or reject it completely.

Hum Hain Rahi Pyar Ke was one of the biggest hits of 1993. It was also well-received on the home video sales front. 'Ghunghat Ki Aad Se' became extremely popular. Alka Yagnik won the National Award for the song and I received my third Filmfare award.

Movie: *Hum Hain Rahi Pyar Ke* | Lyrics: Sameer |
Singers: Kumar Sanu, Alka Yagnik |
Music: Nadeem–Shravan

9

'Ole, Ole, Ole'

1994

Did you know that the very popular song 'Ole, Ole, Ole' had a connection with Mughal Emperor Akbar's navratan Tansen?

Yeh Dillagi (1994) was a superhit film produced by Yash Chopra and directed by Naresh Malhotra. It had Akshay Kumar, Saif Ali Khan and Kajol as the leads. My first film with Yash Chopra was the Jackie Shroff and Juhi Chawla starrer *Aaina* (1993), which had turned out to be a big hit. Post that, I was signed on for the film, *Yeh Dillagi*.

With the great success of *Aashiqui*, Hindi cinema had returned to its romantic era, and the Bollywood music industry stayed on its zenith for the entire decade. In this golden era of music, we were blessed with amazing singers like Udit Narayan, Kumar Sanu, along with music directors like Nadeem–Shravan and A.R. Rehman, to name a few. Another successful music director duo of the same period was Dilip Sen and Sameer Sen, who had mesmerized people with their marvelously composed semi-classical Bollywood numbers.

Dilip was the son of Jamal Sen, a great musician, while Sameer was the son of Dilip's brother Shambhu Sen. A forefather of the Sen family, Kesari Sen, was once a disciple of Tansen and that's why Yash Chopra used to call Dilip Sen

'Tansen'. Initially, Dilip wanted to become a dancer. Sameer, who had learned classical singing from his father, wanted to become a singer. However, destiny had other plans for both of them.

Both Dilip and Sameer's career started with the Hindi film *Surma Bhopali* (1988), which was directed by the comedian Jagdeep. One day, Yash Chopra met them and signed them for *Aaina*.

The success of *Aaina* brought Dilip and Sameer to national prominence. Yash Chopra signed them once again for *Yeh Dillagi*, showing his confidence in the two of them. Meanwhile, I was given the responsibility of writing the songs.

We were making songs one after the other, according to plot of the film, but Yash Chopra had instructed us not to use 'I love you' or similar clichéd phrases in the songs. (The film went on to have an 'I love you' song, but that story is for another day.) If you've been asked not to use such an important phrase directly, that too in a romantic film, it would become a big challenge. Owing to such limitations, we remained stuck for some time.

One day, after a music session, we had all left for our homes. Suddenly, rain gods poured from above, along with a heavy hailstorm. Dilip and Sameer would tell me later that Dilip, who had been driving the car, saw the hailstones which are called *ole* in Hindi. He mumbled 'Ole, Ole' with a smile on his face, and started humming and tapping his fingers on the steering wheel of the car. After reaching home, they called me for an urgent music sitting. I was surprised since we had just met and had discussed the music with the producer. Now they wanted to see me again!

I called them over to my place.

'Tell me Dilip, what do you want to discuss?' I asked him.

'We've got the indirect word for "I love you",' Dilip replied with excitement.

'What's that?' I said eagerly.

'Ole Ole,' he replied with a mischievous grin.

'What does that mean?' I asked with frustration and confusion.

Instead of replying, Dilip and Sameer started thumping my centre table as a dholak and began singing, 'Ole, Ole-Ole… Ole, Ole-Ole.'

I loved the line, but still wanted to know the meaning of the word 'ole'.

'Brother, this is great, but what is this "ole"?' I asked him.

'While driving home there was a hailstorm. In our Rajasthan, we call hail "ole",' he responded.

This made me laugh.

I loved the line and requested them to keep singing till prompted otherwise. They again began thumping on the table and singing. After few minutes, I was blessed with the line, '*Jab bhi koi ladki dekhun mera dil diwana bole, ole, ole-ole… ole, ole-ole.*' Thus, the superhit song of *Yeh Dillagi* was born. Along with 'Ole, Ole, Ole', we had also composed two other songs for Yash Chopra to choose from.

Next day, Dilip and Sameer presented all three songs to Yash Chopra. The first two songs were rejected. They then presented the third one to him. Yash ji loved the song. This song was 'Ole, Ole, Ole'.

'Tansen, this is going to be the biggest hit song of the year,' Yash Chopra said to Dilip with great confidence.

'Sameer, where did the phrase "ole-ole" come from?' Yash ji asked me.

I told him that it was Dilip's suggestion.

'I knew that only a madman like him could come up with such phrases,' he laughed.

The composition and lyrics were ready but the problem was picking the singer. Yash Chopra's favourite singer was Udit Narayan, but I argued that the song would not go with his voice. Someone suggested Abhijeet's name and he was then called to dub it. Abhijeet did a great job, and we later felt that nobody else could have done a better job. On the screen, Saif performed it with equal fervour.

After its release, the film was a smash hit at the box office and the 'Ole, Ole, Ole' song became one of the reasons for the film's success. This movie established Saif Ali Khan as a bankable hero in Bollywood, and it turned out to be Akshay Kumar's second major hit after *Khiladi* (1992).

The youth loved the song across the country. Unfortunately, the song began to be used to tease women. We had heard that in many cities, police had to ban playing of the song near girl's colleges.

So, this is how the song 'Ole, Ole, Ole' was made, indeed casually. People often ask me what it means, and then I laugh and say it means the same as 'Eena Meena Deka'—essentially, nothing.

Movie: ***Yeh Dillagi*** | Lyrics: **Sameer** | Singer: **Abhijeet Bhattacharya** | Music: **Dilip Sen–Sameer Sen**

∽

10

'Main Toh Raste Se Ja Raha Tha'

1995

Coolie No. 1, a Bollywood film made in 1995, changed both the direction and the condition of our film industry. It was the most successful film of that year. The film is arguably counted among the cults and the classics of Hindi film industry. Prior to this film, the duo of director David Dhawan and actor Govinda had done many successful films like *Aankhen* (1993), *Shola Aur Shabnam* (1992), *Raja Babu* (1994), etc., and seeing these two together, people would wait for yet another superhit film and its melodious songs.

It was producer Vashu Bhagnani's first film, and went on to become actress Karisma Kapoor's first successful film at the box office. The music of *Coolie No. 1* became a trendsetter, and the Hindi film industry was flooded with item songs thereafter. The songs from this film have very interesting stories behind their composition. Let me tell the rollercoaster tale of its most successful song, 'Main Toh Raste Se Ja Raha Tha'.

In the film, Govinda was playing the role of a young, fun-loving but poor coolie. All the songs in the film were supposed to be fun songs. Musician duo Anand–Milind and I had completed several songs and had invited the producer, director and the owners of Tips Industries Limited, the music record label that was the distributer of the film, for a music session at a suburban studio. Director David Dhawan, along with Kumar Taurani and Ramesh Taurani of Tips Industries turned up to hear the songs. As we played the song, '*Main toh raste ja raha tha, main to bhel poori kha raha tha*', Ramesh and Kumar started laughing. We all saw their reaction but could not make up our minds as to what to feel about their reaction. The moment the song was over, both of them got up and started leaving without giving any feedback. I understood that they did not like the song.

David had gotten pretty upset seeing their conduct. 'Let's wait for Vashu Bhagnani. He is coming in some time,' David asked them politely.

Both of them sat down and we all started waiting for Vashu ji.

He arrived soon after. I was meeting him after quite a while. We played the song; he listened to it very carefully. The constant grin on his face was a big relief for us. As soon as the song was over, he turned to us saying, 'Very nice song. I like it.'

After we had talked for a while, Vashu ji asked to be excused from the sitting since he had to go for another meeting.

As he left, Taurani brothers gave their unexpected feedback. It was understood that both had waited to see Vashu ji's feedback first. Perhaps they both had felt that Vashu Bhagnani too would not like this song and would reject. But since that is not what had happened, they felt they *had* to make themselves heard.

'What a song you guys have made!' Ramesh dropped a bomb with his unenthusiastic reaction and made fun of the lyrics: '*Main toh raste se ja raha tha, bhelpuri kha raha tha, ladki ghuma raha tha. Tumko mirchi lagi to main kya karoon.*'

'Is this a song or a joke? It sounds like a crass *sadakchaap* song.' Kumar Taurani's reaction was even more hostile.

'Try something else, this will definitely not do,' Ramesh gave us an ultimatum.

After showcasing their heart-breaking reaction for all of us to bear, the Taurani brothers left the studio. We were all extremely distressed by their criticism. David's face turned red with anger upon seeing their behaviour.

'Don't worry, brothers. I swear by this song, if this is dropped, I won't do this film.' David assured us and left the studio.

I could understand why the Taurani brothers were thinking like that. It was a clash between creatives and businessmen. David Dhawan and we were looking at it with a creative eye, while Tauranis as the owners of a music label might have felt that this song was not safe from a business perspective. Instead of an experimental fun song like this, they were probably looking for romantic songs like the ones in *Aashiqui* (1990) and *Saajan* (1991), which could have a longer shelf life and a bigger chance to succeed.

After a few days, there was a meeting in the Taurani brothers' office in which David put his foot down and said that he wanted the song in the movie. Ramesh relented a little and gave him a go-ahead to shoot the song. He told them that once the song sequence was ready it could be decided what was to be done with it. This may seem like good news, but to us it meant that the sword was still hanging over the song till the very end.

The next problem in our list was who would sing this song. Anand–Milind's favourite singer was Udit Narayan, who used to sing almost all their songs. But, this time, we did not agree to his name. After much thought, we decided that it should be sung by Kumar Sanu, who was known for singing only soft romantic compositions and had never sung such an item number. When Kumar Sanu heard the track, he was thankful to us for choosing him for such a fun song.

'You have sung so many romantic songs in your career. We believe that with this one your fans will get to see a new side of you. We are sure they will appreciate it,' I said to him.

Kumar Sanu could see this song's bright future, which is why he sang it wholeheartedly to break the monotony in his discography. When Tauranis heard that Kumar Sanu was the one to have sung 'Main Toh Raste Se Ja Raha Tha', they both were sure that this song would be the reason for the film's failure.

After its release, *Coolie No. 1* turned out to be a super-duper hit at the box office, and the song 'Main Toh Raste Se Ja Raha Tha' became one of the main reasons and selling selling points behind the film's success. Govinda was chosen as the 'Star of the Decade' by Star Screen Awards in their 'Special Jury' category for such an iconic performance.

A few months after the success of the film, I visited Kumar Taurani's house. His grandmother had passed away and I had to pay my condolences. When I held his hand and offered words of sympathy, he tried being cheerful and reminded me of this incident in a light-hearted manner. He said, 'You had written "*teri nani mari to main kya karoon*", and see my nani died!' He laughed and hugged me. All animosity was forgotten in that instant.

Movie: *Coolie No. 1* | Lyrics: Sameer | Singers: Kumar Sanu, Alka Yagnik | Music: Anand-Milind

11

'Yaara O Yaara'

1996

This is not only true for our film industry, it seems to be a general trend across all professions. The people you start your professional career with, after some time, you tend to leave all those companions behind. With each step of growth, you make new friends, happily marching forward on your journey with them. But this rule is flipped over when it comes to me and the famous film producer Sajid Nadiadwala. From his first feature *Zulm Ki Hukumat* released in 1992 to *Housefull 4* (2019), I've written songs for almost all of his films. And the main reason for this bonding is our good rapport and solemn respect for each other.

In the '90s, many music directors were doing wonderfully well, but if you ask anyone today, they will most probably tell you that that the entire decade belonged to the music director duo of Nadeem–Shravan. In those days, music lovers eagerly waited for their new songs, while every big producer of the Hindi film industry wanted to work with them.

In 1996, Sajid Nadiadwala had announced his fourth film to be titled *Jeet*, starring Sunny Deol, Salman Khan and Karisma Kapoor. Like most film producers, Sajid too wanted to work with Nadeem–Shravan.

'Bhaijaan, let's go and meet Sajid Nadiadwala,' I told Nadeem Bhai.

Nadeem—the musical genius—was a very good man at heart, but he was very stubborn too. 'If Sajid wants to work with us, why doesn't he call us himself?' Nadeem responded back.

The next day, I had a meeting with Sajid, who was confused about who should be taken as the music director for his next film. That's when I said to him, 'Bhai Sajid, if you want good songs and good food, you should work with Nadeem–Shravan.'

'Sameer ji, you spoke my heart. In fact, I have been thinking the same for the past few days, but how can I make it possible?' Sajid asked me as if he was working on the formula for world peace.

'Very simple! Just pick up the phone and dial his number,' I said casually.

He immediately called Nadeem. The conversation between both of them was positive and friendly from both sides, and the meeting was fixed for the very next day.

'Okay, tomorrow we'll be there at your Versova bungalow,' Nadeem said to Sajid.

But Sajid interrupted him and spoke frankly, 'No, *I'll* come to your house at Bombay Central if you promise two things: a fantastic music sitting and finger-licking biryani.'

Both of them laughed a lot and promised to meet the next day.

I was happy that I became the reason to introduce two good people. The next day, after having lip-smacking biryani, Sajid spoiled Nadeem's mood by saying, 'Nadeem Bhai, give me a romantic number, I want Sunny Deol to dance on that song.'

'What, Sunny and dance?' Nadeem asked with a shocked expression on his face.

'Yes, I'm serious,' Sajid answered coolly.

Whenever Nadeem–Shravan came across a subject they resonated with, they poured their heart and soul into creating the songs. It mattered little whether the song was filmed on Ajay Devgn or Sunny Deol, as their passion for crafting music remained unwavering. Their favoured genre was the love triangle romantic drama, which allowed them to explore a wide range of emotions. In such dramas, they could delve into the initial meeting with the beloved, the euphoria of being loved and the heart-wrenching moments of separation, among others. This rich tapestry of emotions served as the driving force behind their ability to produce exceptional music.

Nadeem–Shravan and I sat together and all the songs of the film sounded great, but the Sunny Deol dance number was just not happening. One day, during our sitting, when we were trying to work on the Sunny Deol dance number, Shravan started laughing. When we asked the reason behind his laughter, he chuckled and said, 'Bhai, I don't know if Sunny knows how to dance or not, but we have definitely forgotten the art of making songs.'

Something about Shravan's statement incited a challenge in Nadeem. He sat down on the floor and declared, 'I will not get up until I make a song for Sunny today.'

He also pulled me to the floor. Looking serious, he said, 'Pandit ji! Yaar, please write a song for my friend Sunny.'

We all sat down, and Nadeem started to play an amazing tune on the harmonium. The vibe had been created. A few words just tumbled out of my mouth: *'Yaara o yaara'*.

That's it! That's what we needed. From there on words just flowed, and soon the song was completed. This was not a Nadeem–Shravan trademark ghazal song but a completely different style from their previous hit numbers. Since the song was entirely unusual, it had no scope for Kumar Sanu, their favourite singer to sing it.

Nadeem had a unique style of working, in that he would first compose the tune and then, on that composition, he would himself sing in the voice of some prominent singers of that time, only to find out which singer's voice would fit on that particular song. Before giving the super hit song 'Dekha Hai Pehli Baar' to S.P. Balasubrahmanyam, Nadeem had mimicked his voice so well that when Bala heard the recording, he was utterly confused, wondering when had he recorded it.

Singer Vinod Rathod at that time was well-liked due to his songs in successful films like *Chandni* (1989), *Baazigar* (1993), *Darr* (1993) and *Khalnayak* (1993), and he was chosen for this song. Vinod sang it brilliantly with Alka Yagnik.

My friend Raj Kanwar, who was directing this film, shot this song beautifully in green and snow-covered valleys. Sunny tied a scarf on his head and surprised his fans with his unique dance with Karisma Kapoor, immortalizing the song. 'Yaara O Yaara' proved to be the biggest song of the film and one of the most successful songs of the year. To some extent, the credit for the creation and success of this song also goes to the biryani that pulled Sajid towards Nadeem–Shravan.

Every film or song that remains in the minds of people mainly stays due to its music video. Even today, if you listen to this song on the radio, you'll remember Sunny Deol stomping his feet on the ground as if he were killing insects. I give my heartfelt appreciation to the only film director in Bollywood who could get Sunny to dance—the late Raj Kanwar.

Movie: *Jeet* | Lyrics: **Sameer** | Singers: **Vinod Rathod, Alka Yagnik** | Music: **Anu Malik**

∽

12

'Pardesi Pardesi Jana Nahi'

1996

It was the year 1995. Dushmani (1995) and Raja Hindustani (1996) were two films that famous producers Morani Brothers were making at the same time. In terms of budget and star cast, *Dushmani* was a much bigger film than *Raja Hindustani* for the makers. Expectedly, there was less focus on the smaller film. I knew this because I was writing lyrics for both the films.

Dharmesh Darshan was signed to direct *Raja Hindustani*. Aamir Khan and Karisma Kapoor were chosen to play the leads.

The story that was narrated to me was a typical formulaic story where a poor taxi driver Raja falls in love with a super-rich girl who marries Raja against her parents' wishes. Later, her parents try to create differences between the couple.

After listening to the story, I felt as if I had got the wish of my heart because a song 'Pardesiyon Se Na Akhiyan Milana' from *Jab Jab Phool Khile* (1965) written by my favourite lyricist Anand Bakshi was in my mind since my youth. I had always thought that if I ever got a chance, I would write a song just like that. Now had come the time, and I realized that this movie needed a song with that mood.

I will always remember the music sittings for this film.

Ramesh Taurani and Kumar Taurani, the owners of the music label Tips Industries, along with Aamir Khan, Karisma Kapoor, Nadeem–Shravan and I used to sit together and discuss the upcoming film's music. We were all super excited for this film.

The sound track was being worked on, but we had got stuck on a very emotional moment in the film where the hero was getting separated from the heroine.

'Pandit ji, let us do something heart-touching here,' Nadeem said to me excitedly.

Nadeem–Shravan had composed an excellent tune that inspired me to take my favourite song 'Pardesiyon Se Na Akhiyan Milana' forward. I wrote, '*pardesi pardesi jana nahi*'. To me, it was a nice hook line. It was complementing the tune as well as the story. So, I finished the lyrics and handed it to Nadeem and Shravan. We were now ready with the tune and lyrics to take it to the recording stage. Udit Narayan and Alka Yagnik, who were chosen to give their voices to this song, went ahead and expressively sang it.

We were excited to present it to the makers and actors. And when we did, like we had expected, everyone loved the song! That's when I realized that Kumar Taurani was trying to say something. He had a strange objection to one of the words.

'Pardesi is sounding like *purrrr*-desi. It sounds vulgar.' Kumar ji was critical.

'Yeah, it sounds indecent. People will laugh a lot on hearing it.' Ramesh Taurani was even more critical, just like he had been for 'Main Toh Raste Se Ja Raha Tha'.

Upon hearing their criticism, everyone present there realized that the word and the way it was being sung sounded like a case of flatulence—in simpler words, a fart. We all felt that everyone had got so carried away by the flow of music that we did not think that we had written something that might sound inappropriate. Well, now we were all in agreement with the Tauranis that we had made a mistake. But the question was what to do next.

'Let's write something new,' Kumar Taurani said bluntly and laughed.

'Of course, we can't take this song to the audiences,' Ramesh Taurani was firm.

'But I want this word "pardesi" because it suits the story and my tune,' said Nadeem, confident in the lyrics.

'The hero lives in the hills, and today, he is leaving the heroine and going back forever. There can be no better line than *"pardesi jana nahi, mujhe chod ke",'* Shravan said with conviction.

Nadeem Bhai suggested that he would go ahead and record it with Kumar Sanu; he was of the opinion that it would sound better in his voice. But my opinion was that no matter who sung it, the word was going to sound the same. 'Then, what?' We were all turning to each other to suggest a way out.

'Let's scrap the song,' Sharavan suggested as a last resort.

'No way! This song has the potential to be a super hit!' Nadeem reacted loudly.

'Are you sure?' Kumar Taurani asked Nadeem.

'Yes, I'm sure. It's a beautiful song after all. Let's release the song as it is. If anybody criticizes, I'll take the responsibility.' Nadeem was confident in his creation.

The makers and other team members were impressed by Nadeem Saifi's conviction and assurance. The music session ended with a decision that the song would be released as it is.

After they all left, I suggested to the two music directors, 'What if we don't start the song with "pardesi"? I'll write something else to begin the song with, and maybe this way it won't sound odd.'

Both the music directors loved my proposal. I wrote

a couplet that Nadeem–Shravan recorded with folk singer Sapna Awasthi on the prelude. This was our effort to repair the damage.

After its release, 'Pardesi, Pardesi Jana Nahi' went on to become a major chartbuster at the time, which also led to the film's success. Udit Narayan won his third Filmfare award in the 'Best Playback Singer' category for this song. The album became the bestselling Bollywood soundtrack of the year by a wide margin. *Planet Bollywood* ranked Raja Hindustani's soundtrack at 56 in its list of all-time top 100 greatest Bollywood soundtracks. Every music critic praised the song. It was the third bestselling album of the 1990s, after *Aashiqui* (1990) and *Dil To Pagal Hai* (1997). I felt proud that two of them were written by me.

Trust me, to date nobody has pointed out to me the funny sounding 'Purrrdesi'. During the making of songs, there are many issues we handle that never reach the public. It is my belief that our audience never gets into unnecessary criticism. They just listen to our creation and get entertained.

I say that the magic of Nadeem–Shravan's music had such a surreal impact on the listeners that they couldn't even realize that something they were hearing could have sounded absurd or laughable. I often say that music and God are similar—both cannot be seen. You just feel them from the bottom of your heart.

Movie: *Raja Hindustani* | Lyrics: Sameer |
Singers: Sapna Awasthi, Udit Narayan, Alka Yagnik |
Music: Nadeem–Shravan

13

'Na Na Na Na Re'

1997

There is a very interesting story behind the making of the song 'Na Na Na Na Re'. Almost in every song of mine the punch line of the song has been coined by me, but here the line came from a different source.

During a particular era in Indian cinema, the names of my father, the lyricist Anjaan, and the legendary Amitabh Bachchan were almost synonymous with each other. They together contributed to numerous chart-topping songs in the '70s, '80s and '90s, touching the hearts of countless individuals. Among the many super hit songs of that time, my father penned several unforgettable ones for Amit ji, including 'Khaike Pan Banaras Wala', 'Gori Hain Kalaiyan', 'Dil To Hai Dil', 'Rote Huye Aate Hain Sab', 'Log Kehte Hain Main Sharaabi Hoon', and many others. These collaborations left an indelible mark on the world of Hindi cinema.

Being Anjaan's son, I had always dreamt of working with superstar Amitabh Bachchan, and I thought that it would be great if I could write hit numbers for him too just like my father had. But when I was trying to make a mark in the industry as a lyricist, Amit ji wasn't very active at the time. Some people speculated that he had retired.

One day, I read in the newspapers that Amit ji was making

his comeback in Bollywood with Mehul Kumar's *Mrityudaata* (1997). I crossed my fingers and started hoping that I would get this film somehow. I consider myself fortunate that I was soon called by Anand–Milind to write the music for this film. I was glad to the Almighty, that He had listened to my prayers. I was very excited thinking that I was going to write lyrics for the superstar Amitabh Bachchan.

We started our music sittings, and I sensed that there was tremendous excitement in the entire unit of the movie, including the superstar. Amit ji was very much involved in music compositions and visited all the sessions regularly. Since this was his comeback film, he did not want to leave any stone unturned.

One day, during a music sitting, Amit ji expressed that he had the desire to do a song with Daler Mehdi in this film. He also wanted to shoot a video with him. Everyone liked his suggestion because Daler was a pop sensation at the time. Amit ji took out his phone and immediately called Daler Mehdi in his trademark KBC (Kaun Banega Crorepati) style, '*Hello, main Amitabh Bachchan bol raha hoon*.' He invited him to the music sitting to discuss the project.

Daler Mehdi had come to the music room of Anand–Milind at Khar with his entourage. I was really surprised to see the size of his staff members as he had come with his secretary, guards, managers, etc. Amit ji also used to come with his entire staff for such important meetings.

At the beginning of the music sitting, Daler Paji asked, 'What are we here to discuss? What kind of song do you want me to make?'

Before we could reply, Amit ji said, 'Brother, this is certainly going to be your kind of dance number so it's better that you suggest what we should do.'

Something struck Daler Mehdi. He smiled and said, 'Sir,

I often sing a phrase during my shows, "*Na na na na na re*". If Sameer ji can convert this line into a song then we can compose it as a dance number. I'm sure this will be a sure-shot hit.' He was very confident in his idea.

I asked him to sing this line a couple of times. With his voice in my ears, I closed my eyes in search of words. He kept humming, but once I opened my eyes, I had the complete line on my lips. Pravina Bhardwaj, a writer friend of mine, used to playfully say to me, '*Sadde naal rahoge to aish karoge*' I thought, if I connected this line to 'na na na na na re', it would sound great.

I shared what came to my mind at that time, '*Na na na na re… Sadde naal rahoge to aish karoge, zindagi ke sare maze cash karoge… Sadde naal*'. Everybody jumped in excitement and praised me for my couplet. Amit ji and Daler Paji both ran and hugged me. Anand–Milind immediately composed the song on the harmonium. Everyone was very satisfied with the song, which was already sounding like a hit dance number.

When we were busy working on the song, everyone noticed that Daler Paji's secretary was seeming anxious. After every 15–20 minutes, she would come close to Daler Mehdi to murmur something in private, like they were discussing something serious.

Amit ji couldn't hold himself back from asking why she was going back and forth and interrupting the sessions. His manager briefed him quickly that Daler Mehdi was asking the producers for ₹45 lakh as his fee for this song. Amit ji was stunned to hear such a huge amount just for a dance number in a film, which was double his own fees.

He angrily asked Daler Mehdi to clarify the reason behind his mammoth charges. Daler Mehdi acted as if he didn't know anything about the whole matter. Amit ji explained, 'Look Daler, you're going to get huge publicity worth ₹10–

12 crore after you are seen in the film singing and dancing with Amitabh Bachchan. Ask your manager to deduct 45 lakh from the 10–12 crore and return rest of the money to me for appearing with you in the video. Or else, let's finish off the matter here itself. We'll find someone else.'

There was pin-drop silence. Mehul Kumar was seen holding his head in his hands. I was sure that this song was not going to happen due to an ego clash between the two stars. But Daler had respect for Amit ji. He went up to him and asked him to forgive him and forget the whole matter. 'I'm ready to do the number for you free of cost, Sir,' said Daler.

The matter was resolved by the timely intervention of Amitabh Bachchan. The song was recorded and shot with great enthusiasm. Although the movie didn't do well at the box office, but the song went on to become one of the most popular songs of the year.

Movie: *Mrityudaata* | Lyrics: **Sameer** | Singers: **Sudesh Bhonsle, Daler Mehdi** | Music: **Anand–Milind**

∽

14

'O O Jaane Jaana'

1998

Let's talk about the 1998 song that made people go crazy! 'O O Jaane Jaana' from the Salman Khan and Kajol starrer *Pyar Kiya Toh Darna Kya* (1998) took the nation by storm. Even today, when you listen to this song, two things come to mind: one, the voice of the singer, and the other, a bare-chested Salman Khan who went shirtless for the first time with this song.

Jatin-Lalit and I have produced a number of memorable songs together. I have always had a great experience working with the music-director duo. When we were brought together for this film, director Sohail Khan had briefed us that this song was to be shot on Salman Khan performing on stage. We were also told to keep it as modern as possible.

With this little input from the director as our anchor, we got busy with the song. Jatin–Lalit are considered masters of modernizing a song; you will always find newness in their work. Who can forget the beautiful songs of *Jo Jeeta Wohi Sikandar* (1992), *Khamoshi* (1996), *Kuch Kuch Hota Hai* (1998) and *Mohabbatein* (2000)? Lalit is a master guitarist and always composes his tunes on the guitar. For this song too, the duo composed a great tune, which had an amazing guitar solo. I loved the opening sequence of the music.

I was given the tune for writing my lyrics over it. It was challenging for me, as I had to write lyrics that reflected the freshness of the composition. It took time, but ultimately the poetry that came as a blessing to me sounded fresh:

O O jaane jaana
Dhoondhe tujhe deewana
Sapnon mein roz aaye
Aa zindagi mein aa na

Although I was happy with my writing, I thought it was rather basic. But when I submitted it to the music directors, surprisingly, they appreciated it.

The compositions and lyrics were now ready to go to the next stage where we had to choose a suitable voice. This was the period of very successful singers like Kumar Sanu, Udit Narayan, Abhijeet, etc., and most of the big films used to go to them. We were busy thinking about whose voice would be best-suited for this one. Just then a recommendation for a new voice came from Salman Khan. We all felt that this would be a wrong move and that we were going to spoil it by experimenting away a great tune on a new voice.

This was Salman Khan's friend, Kamaal Khan, a London based pop singer. As a pop singer, Kamaal was very successful in England, which became the reason for his selection to sing in this film. But everyone felt that singing a private album in England and singing playback in Bollywood were two very different things.

'I've already promised him, so we've got to give him this song,' Salman said to Jatin–Lalit.

'What if the public doesn't like his voice?' Lalit was hesitant.

'I don't care,' said Salman, confident about his selection.

Salman Khan's decision was final and we had to record

Kamaal Khan for the most beautiful composition of this film.

Kamaal was called to the studio for a rehearsal. He was very nervous considering that it was not only a big film he was recording for but the song had to be picturized on Salman. Such pressure must have surely been messing with his mind. We made him feel comfortable and asked him to go on the mic. At first, he showed signs of hesitation by asking the recordist to play the music track again, and then again. This initially led us to doubt his ability to render a Bollywood song as a playback singer. But, as soon as he started humming and finally sang the song, everyone present was mesmerized by his delightfully unique voice. We were all pleasantly surprised. It was a fresh and beautiful voice that we were sure the public was going to like. This gave us confidence.

We finished the recording in a couple of sessions. Since Kamaal's background was that of a pop singer, he was unfamiliar with the constraints faced by playback singers. Jatin–Lalit had a tough time grooming Kamaal Khan as a playback singer and dubbing him over the track. But when the song was ready, we were sure that Kamaal was going to be a sensation very soon. The song was now ready to be shot.

It had been decided that the song was to be shot on an open stage at the sea shore, and everyone went to the shoot with the same plan in mind. But on reaching there, I don't know what got into Salman; he took off his jacket and his T-shirt, and gave the first iconic shirtless performance of his career.

On the release of the music, this particular song became a rage. Salman Khan's shirtless look in 'O O Jaane Jaana' drove the nation crazy. How can anyone forget Salman Khan's eye-catching appearance wearing blue ripped jeans? A new era began where young stars started copying Salman Khan and started doing similar characters and performances. 'O O Jaane

Jaana' topped the chart of the year. Kamaal Khan became an icon overnight. The media was stunned with Salman's appearance. What more could his fans desire from him! He looked even more attractive than his usual self in the video, bare-chested, with his guitar and ripped jeans.

Pyar Kiya Toh Darna Kya turned out to be a blockbuster, with great performances from both Salman and Kajol. The soundtrack went on to sell over 10 million copies and the huge success of the movie has widely been attributed by film pundits to the popularity of Kamaal's debut song. That year, Kamaal received the most prestigious Filmfare's 44th R.D. Burman Award, conferred on an upcoming musical talent, for singing 'O O Jaane Jaana'.

Unfortunately in 2002, as an eye-witness in Salman Khan's hit-and-run case, Kamaal Khan too got caught in the crossfire. This particular incident hampered his career. A rising star could not reach where he should have reached. But who can erase what is written in our fate? Whenever you hear 'O O Jaane Jaana', you cannot help but appreciate Kamal Khan's singing.

Movie: *Pyar Kiya Toh Darna Kya* | Lyrics: Sameer | Singer: Kamaal Khan | Music: Jatin–Lalit

15

'Kuch Kuch Hota Hai'

1998

'Kuch Kuch Hota Hai' was one of the most popular songs of the '90s era. The song had become an anthem for first love.

The years 1997–98 was a time in my life when a large part of my support system came crashing down. My father passed away, my mentor Gulshan Kumar was killed, the owners of Tips music were jailed, Nadeem–Shravan broke up and Nadeem had left India forever. This era was a very difficult phase in my life. I was engulfed in darkness.

When I came back from my ancestral village in Varanasi to Mumbai after performing the last rites of my father, there was no one to hold me with affection. I often felt that my journey in Bollywood had ended because I was considered the lyricist of Nadeem–Shravan, which was perhaps why all the music directors were annoyed with me and no one was ready to give me work.

One day, my mother reminded me that when a door closes, another opens. 'In your case, God Almighty has shut many doors. Have faith in Him, for He is going to open as many doors of opportunity very soon,' she added. To me, it could only have been God who had comforted me in the form of my mother. My mother's words were proven right in the time to come.

A few days later, the first call I received was from the great filmmaker Yash Chopra. He called me to his bungalow for some work. I took my mother's blessings by touching her feet and went to meet Yash Chopra at his house.

'Meet Karan Johar. He is making a film. I want you to write songs for him.' Yash Chopra introduced me to Karan.

I congratulated him for his first movie as a director and asked him the title of the film.

'*Kuch Kuch Hota Hai*,' Karan replied.

Only later did I come to know that Javed Akhtar had been called in to write the lyrics for the film before me, but Javed Sahab had refused the offer, saying, 'I do not like the title of the film.' Yash Chopra had then placed two options in front of Karan Johar—Anand Bakshi or Sameer.

'I want to work with the young lyricist with fresh thoughts, so I would like to meet Sameer ji,' Karan Johar had said to Yash ji.

Karan Johar gave me two hours of detailed narration of his film. A narration in which all the department heads of his unit—from the cameraman to custome designer to art director—everyone was present there. This was the most unique experience of my life.

I came back home and started thinking about the songs. I thought that if Karan had called Javed Akhtar first, then he would definitely want good poetry. So for the first time in my career, I moved away from my regular style and wrote some very deep poetry, by using difficult Urdu words. After writing the mukhda full of Urdu poetry, I went to present it to Karan with confidence.

Zulfon ke saaye, rukh pe giraaye,
Shaidaai mere dil ko banaaye,
Shabanam ke moti pal pal pirota hai,
Kya karun haye kuch kuch hota hai

Karan went silent for two minutes after listening to these lines. 'Sameer ji, I asked you to write my songs considering you are a young man, but you are sounding older than Majrooh Sahab and Anand Bakshi Sahab.' Karan looked disappointed while talking to me.

'Then?' I was clueless while replying to him.

'Sir, don't take any pressure. Just write very simple poetry.' Karan was very clear about what he wanted from me.

I came home with a heavy heart and thought that this film was going to be taken away from me. I was absolutely blank and could not understand what to write for *Kuch Kuch Hota Hai*, and wrote a few lines while trying to put a reign on my poetic instincts.

Tum paas aaye, yun muskuraye
Tum ne na jane kya, sapne dikhaye
Ab to mera dil, jaage na sota hai
Kya karoon haye, kuch kuch hota hai

I was very confused whether these were good lines—' 'simple poetry', as Karan had wanted—or if they were too simple. I didn't know whether Karan was going to like it or not. I will admit—if I were to be asked—I did not like what I had written. I had written something else too, which I had decided to present as a last resort.

However, it never came to that. As soon as I read these lines to Karan, I still remember he had jumped from one sofa to another in happiness. He loved my poetry!

'Sir, this is what I wanted from you!' he said to me with a wide smile on his face.

'I can write better than this if you say,' I spluttered out.

'Sir, please don't confuse me. I've got what I wanted.' He seemed sure.

I could see from Karan's response how sharp this man was and how clear in his thoughts. I remember thinking to myself that this young man was going to last a long time in Bollywood.

Lata Mangeshkar was approached to sing the song but she requested Yash ji that someone else be given the chance instead of her, and therefore Alka Yagnik was selected for the female voice and Udit Narayan as the male singer. Udit Narayan had a habit of getting very nervous just before a recording. He would make several funny excuses till the time he came to the microphone, which is when his genius emerged. Both the singers had electric chemistry, and it shows on the track.

After the music was released, it became a rage and the film was a smash hit at the box office. My fans from all over the world loved and praised my songs, but the most beautiful compliment I received was from the famous film director (Late) Raj Kanwar.

'Sameer ji, all your songs are amazing but the title track is the best. I loved "haai" in the line "Kya karoon haai kuch kuch hota hai". This "haai" outshines your entire song.' Raj Kanwar offered these generous words of appreciation to me.

A few months ago, some people from BBC London had come to interview me. They told me that a list of 100 years of best musical cinema was being prepared. I was delighted to learn from them that 'your *Kuch Kuch Hota Hai*' was being given a place in this list. Such recognition always encourages one to give their best and leave everything else to destiny.

Movie: *Kuch Kuch Hota Hai* | Lyrics: Sameer | Singers: Alka Yagnik, Udit Narayan | Music: Jatin-Lalit

16

'Soldier, Soldier'

1998

Although I had written most of my songs for Nadeem–Shravan and experienced most success in the 1990s, filmmakers and producers wanted to try different permutations and create a music production team as per their choice. Every now and then, they would pair me up with a different composer, and sometimes they would bring a different lyricist to work with Nadeem–Shravan. Something similar happened with the Bobby Deol and Preity Zinta starrer *Soldier*, which was released in 1998.

I was at the peak of my career in 1998 and was entering a successful phase as an established lyricist in the industry. That year, I had signed on a total of 18 big productions, and that much work was enough to keep any lyricist very busy, with little time for much else.

One day, I got a call from Nadeem.

'Samrat, we were offered a good film, but I said no to it,' said Nadeem as soon as I picked up the phone. Alongside his many other nicknames for me, Nadeem also used to fondly call me Samrat.

'Why, Bhaijaan?' I asked, curious about why Nadeem would call me simply to convey that he had rejected a project.

'Because there was a condition with the film offer,' Nadeem replied.

My curiosity got the better of me. I wanted to know which film was he talking about, who was the producer and most of all why was Nadeem Bhai being so mysterious about it. 'Bhaijaan, why did you decline the film, please tell me the whole story,' I asked him politely because I knew that any kind of irritation on my part would give ammunition to Nadeem Bhai, for he loved to engage in banter and take the mickey out of me.

Nadeem was grave in his response, 'Because the Tauranis are trying to break our team. They want us to work with Javed Akhtar and not with you for this new film, *Soldier*.' Having worked with the Taurani brothers before, I said that it was impossible they would do such a thing.

After listening to the whole story, I calmed down and explained to him that our team was not dependent on anyone's mercy, and whoever works with us has always enjoyed the success of hit songs in their film. We need not be insecure about our position in the industry. Considering that Javed Sahab is undoubtedly a legendary lyricist, I tried convincing Nadeem that he must take this opportunity and that it would be a great project to work on. I told him that I firmly believed that work comes not only by making a team or having talent but also from luck. I told Nadeem that perhaps this film was not in my destiny. After a lot of persuasion, Nadeem Bhai agreed, and the team of Nadeem–Shravan and Javed Akhtar took the responsibility of *Soldier's* (1998) music.

The team started on their music sessions. There were a lot of creative differences between Nadeem Bhai and Javed Sahab, but both were professional about it and kept their differences aside. The trio worked hard over the next few months and came up with two songs.

Some time later, I went to Javed Sahab's house and found him very unhappy with Nadeem Saifi. 'Brother, your music directors are very strange people. After the making of two good songs, they say that some songs will be written by Javed Sahab and some songs will be written by Sameer. Please tell them this is not done,' said Javed Akhtar with great displeasure.

It was a very strange situation for me; I could not understand what to do about it. While I did not like interfering in other people's projects, even if they were my closest friends, I had great respect for Javed Sahab and could not turn down his earnest request.

With a lot of hesitation, I called Nadeem with the intention of making a compromise between the two greats and put the phone on speaker, so that Javed Sahab could listen to our conversation.

Nadeem Bhai is a very intelligent man. He understood that I was with Javed Sahab. After listening to me, he gave a few words of assurance, 'Don't worry, Samrat. I will do as you say.' This seemed to calm Javed Sahab. After that day, everything went on according to plan. But something else was written in the fate of this film.

An incident that shook the entire nation was the murder of music mogul Gulshan Kumar ji, which happened around the same time as the making of this film. Unfortunately, Nadeem's name cropped up in the murder investigation and he and film producer Ramesh Taurani were jailed. The movie *Soldier* almost died because all the key people related to this film were in jail. For me, this was the worst time in the Hindi film industry.

But time is the biggest healer. Eventually, when Ramesh Taurani was released from jail after a month, he decided to resume the making of the film. He kept the first schedule of filming in Switzerland. The responsibility of song composition was now given to Anu Malik, and Ramesh Taurani went to Javed Sahab requesting him to write the songs immediately, as the production had already been delayed.

'Okay, when would you like to receive these songs?' asked Javed Sahab.

'Sir, here is the thing. My film unit is shooting in Switzerland, and I have to send all six songs for shooting within six days. If I do not do this, I will suffer a huge loss,' Ramesh ji openly confided in Javed Sahab about the problems he was facing.

'So you want me to write the lyrics of six songs in six days?' Javed Sahab was flabbergasted at the demand, something he had not seen in his long and storied career so far.

'Yes, Sir,' Ramesh Taurani replied in a slow but optimistic tone.

'Brother, I write Hindi film songs, not ad-film jingles. It takes me more than six days to think of just one song. I am of the opinion that you should work with a new lyricist who can write songs for you as per your demand.' Javed Sahab excused himself from the film and from working with the people associated with it.

Both Taurani brothers came out of his home with great disappointment. They immediately called Anu Malik and told him everything. Anu Malik suggested my name to them, and everyone came to my place at once. After listening to the whole story, I felt that these people were in deep trouble. After all the legal troubles, if this film wouldn't release, the Tauranis were looking at not just a huge loss but possibly losing their entire film business altogether. They looked heart broken.

Seeing all this, I made up my mind that I must help them. Anu and I accepted the challenge and we both went to a Lonavala resort to complete the task.

Now, the challenge for me was to write a romantic song

keeping the title of the film in my mind. As a word, 'soldier' is a rather unromantic, or even an unpoetic word. Coming up with combinations for a song using this word was proving to be tough. I wracked my brains for several hours trying to come up with something.

But someone has rightly said that those who try hard are never defeated. I finally arrived at the lyrics of the title song after quite a struggle:

Soldier, Soldier
Meethi batein bolkar,
Dil ko chura le gaya.

Anu and the Tauranis loved the lyrics. After composing the title song, we knew what kind of songs we now had to make for the film. So, Anu Malik and I stayed together for a few days at the resort; I wrote while he composed. And then one day, we walked into a studio with the determination to come out only after having recorded all the songs in that album. We recorded all the six songs in a single sitting in a studio in Mumbai and handed over six songs within six days to Ramesh ji.

The title song of the film became smashing hit. Thankfully, the film too was received well at the box office. After so many years, when I met Nadeem Bhai in London, he recalled this film and said, 'You were right, Sameer. Work does not come only by making a team or having talent but also from luck. *Soldier* was in your destiny, and despite so many ups and downs, it finally came to only you. Those Tauranis wanted to keep you out of this project, but you were the one who ended up saving them!'

Movie: *Soldier* | Lyrics: Sameer | Singers: Kumar Sanu, Alka Yagnik | Music: Anu Malik

17

'*Suno Gaur Se Duniya Walon*'

1998

Bollywood film director and producer Mukul Anand, the maker of multi-starrer films, was known for his stylish film-making. After the success of *Agneepath* (1990), *Hum* (1991) and *Khuda Gawah* (1992), he wanted to make a star-studded film with a huge star cast. This most ambitious project was titled *Dus*. Vinod Khanna, Sanjay Dutt, Salman Khan, Raveena Tandon, Shilpa Shetty, amongst many others, were cast in the film. Just after its announcement, the film became one of the most-awaited titles of the year.

As a lyricist, I had worked with Mukul Anand and had a great working relationship with him. One day, he called me to talk about *Dus*.

'Sameer ji! I'm going to make the biggest film of my career,' said the director excitedly.

He had great expectations from me and wanted me to write a patriotic song. 'Will you write an anthem for me?' asked Mukul.

'Rabindranath Tagore has already written an anthem; why do you want me to write it again?' I asked both in curiosity and in jest.

He laughed and replied, 'I want an anthem for the youth of India.'

His response disconcerted me a little more. 'Why? Isn't our youth singing the national anthem?' I said, hiding my confusion in a bit of banter.

Mukul understood my sense of humour. He smiled first but then said with a grim face, 'For 50 years, we've been listening to the same old patriotic songs on 26 January or 15 August. I want to give the youth something new to listen to, and I want every Indian to sing this song.' He asked me to pen down an energetic and patriotic song that could inspire the youth of India.

I asked, 'Can you explain what exactly you are trying to show in the film through this song?' I wanted to see how Mukul had visualized it.

He closed his eyes and started briefing me, 'I want to feature the prime minister of India, Lata Mangeshkar, Sachin Tendulkar and so many big stars of this continent, all talking about harmony brotherhood, patriotism, and such things.' He told me that this song in his imagination would start from Wankhede Stadium where Sachin Tendulkar would be standing at the centre of the stadium with people cheering, shouting and waving the national flag. From there, Sachin would start singing the song, and this is how it would begin.

I had written so many songs and had worked with so many people by then, but Mukul appeared as the biggest admirer of my pen and my writing. I felt blessed that he had called me to write a song of his choice leaving behind great lyricists, like Gulzar Sahab, Javed Sahab, Majrooh Sahab, Anand Bakshi, and other greats in that league.

I was known for my romantic songs and it was indeed very tough to write something as powerful as Kavi Pradeep's verses, such as 'Aye Mere Watan Ke Logon', 'Door Hato Aye Duniya Walon', 'De Di Humein Azadi', etc. But I took it as a challenge and started working on the song.

After the brief, I came back to my home and started thinking what to write. It took me a long time to pen down the desired lines. I was in the process of writing and deleting lines constantly.

One day, Mukul Anand called me to his office. He wanted to introduce three new music directors who were from an ad-film background. Mukul Anand was also a very famous ad filmmaker. He introduced me to Shankar–Ehsaan–Loy and asked if I was fine working with new music directors. I have always believed in talent and was open to working with new ones even though I was a big name by then. They were very humble and looked quite talented.

'Sir, we all are big fan of yours,' said Ehsaan.

'It is a big opportunity for us to work with you and Mukul Sir,' Shankar added.

After that meeting, I came back to my home but I was in search of that first line that was supposed to be the mukhda of the song. But nothing was coming to my mind. *What should be the correct line? What should be the correct word?* I kept thinking about it through the day.

A couple of days later, I was sitting with my friends and we were discussing about the cricket teams of different countries. Some of them were praising Australia, some of them were praising Pakistan, but I said, '*Theek hai, woh log bhi achche hain. Lekin apne Hindustani sabse aage hain* (That's all right, they too are good. But us Indians are far ahead).'

I realize that I think this was the line I was looking for. *Sabse aage Hindustani.* I immediately left from there to work on the song and started writing the mukhda. Finally I had the hook line: 'Sabse Aage Honge Hindustani'. After zeroing in on the first line, I started writing the mukhda and finished it as:

Suno gaur se duniya walon,
Buri nazar na humpe daalo,
Chahe jitna zor laga lo,
Sabse aage honge hindustani.

I was very excited, so I immediately called the composers and said, 'Guys, I think I have the song with me now.' They wanted to hear the song over the phone, but I refused and asked to meet them the next morning.

Next morning, they all were waiting for me to narrate the mukhda. I sang the line, and all three loved it and swiftly got to working on the compositions. We were ready by the evening and presented the song to Mukul. He heard the song thrice and looked at us; we were nervous. He hugged all of us in joy, saying, 'Guys, this is the song I was looking for.'

Mukul loved the song so much, he announced that while the budget of the film was ₹6 crore, he was allocating ₹8 crore only for this song.

His confidence over the song put pressure on us, so we started working hard on it and wanted it to be the biggest song of the year. The composition and lyrics were ready for recording after ten days of hard work. Shankar Mahadevan sang the song incredibly well in his powerful voice. Mukul Anand started shooting for the film, and soon enough magazines and newspapers were covering *Dus*. But God had other plans.

One morning, we heard that Mukul Anand had passed away due to cardiac arrest. Everyone was shattered by this news. We had recorded three songs for *Dus* by the time of the shoot in the USA. The film was shelved after his death.

After some time, T-Series, the producers of the film, shot an album with Sanjay Dutt and Salman Khan. The song that was supposed to be done in ₹8 crore was shot with a small budget on Juhu beach with a few stars and the crowd waving the national flag in their hands. Regardless, the song became an instant hit.

One day, as I was passing through Kachchh in Gujarat, I saw a couple of young policemen singing and dancing on this particular song. Looking at them, it seemed true that what Mukul Anand had wanted from this song had become a reality. I looked towards the sky and prayed for his soul.

Song: 'Suno Gaur Se Duniya Walon' | Lyrics: Sameer | Singers: Shankar Mahadevan, Udit Narayan, Mahalakshmi Iyer, Domnique | Music: Shankar-Ehsaan-Loy

18

'Kisi Disco Mein Jaaye'

1998

B*ade Miyan Chote Miyan* (1998) was a much talked of about film of its time. The two biggest film stars of the time, Amitabh Bachchan and Govinda, whose fans were eager to see them together, were both featured in this film. Bringing mega stars together is a mammoth task for a filmmaker. Not only is their huge fee a big issue, but their dates, demands (sometimes, tantrums) and egos have to be handled very carefully. And all this can be managed only by an experienced and reputed producer like Vashu Bhagnani and a super hit director like David Dhawan who were at the top of their career and in a position to overcome such challenges.

All of David's films are known for their excellent comedy and wonderful music. David did not have the music director of his choice in this film. Music director Viju Shah came highly recommended. Both Amitabh Bachchan and a financier of Vashu ji had promoted him. And this was enough to make a director like David, who liked to stick to his team, his actor and his winning combination, rather restless. He was sure that his film's music was going to be the worst of his career.

My rapport with David was very good. This is why both Amitabh Bachchan and Vashu Bhagnani who knew this entrusted me with the responsibility of preparing David for

Viju Shah. When I met David and asked about the music director of the film, he expressed his displeasure through minced words. 'This film is as much mine as it is of those who are hiring my music director. Of course, they are allowed to bring whoever they want.'

I felt that David was not ready for Viju at all.

'Brother, he has composed very famous songs in the past like "Tu Cheez Badi Hai Mast Mast". I'm sure he will do a good job with our film too,' I reminded David of some of Viju's best works to make him comfortable.

'Sameer, I have no issue with Viju. He is the son of a legendry music director Kalyanji [of the Kalyanji–Anandji duo] and is an expert in his work. I am uncomfortable with him because I have never worked with him before. It is important to know someone personally before working with them,' David clarified his apprehension.

Since I understood David's restlessness, and since I probably had a solution to his problem, I told him, 'David, you leave this to me because I know him personally and I can guarantee that he'll do a great job.'

David was relaxed with my assurance. But the other problem was that Viju's studio was very far from our place. The studio was at Pedder Road and we both lived in Andheri and Juhu. Going to Viju's studio meant our entire day being wasted. Both of us were so busy in our careers at that time that it was absolutely impossible to spend the whole day just for a music sitting. The solution to this problem was bigger than the problem before us.

'If both of us can go to his place very early in the morning before traffic hours and return to our places before noon having finished the music sitting, then we can do other works for the rest of the day,' I said. That day I was to David a *sankatmochan*, the remover of obstacles, who brought solutions to all the problems related to this film. David loved this suggestion too.

'Why don't you go to his place first and meet him. Discuss the lyrics and music first, then I will also join you both,' David made a suggestion. I felt it was quite reasonable, so I nodded in agreement.

My first meeting with Viju was excellent; we discussed the music of the film and other aspects related to it. I told him that David wanted every song in the film to be a super hit item song. I briefed him about David's expectations and apprehensions.

'You don't worry about the songs of the film. Mark my words that people will remember this film because of its songs.' I was very satisfied to see Viju's confidence.

I must say that the process of making a song is very boring. If a non-film person is forced to sit through the process, I'm sure he would run out of the studio scratching his head in frustration. A music director jams with many instrument players and singers and records different sounds, tracks, etc., to create a groove, which a new person will definitely not understand. The person would wonder what exactly is happening in the studio. That is why, a music director usually doesn't allow anyone out of the team during this time in the studio.

After that, we had many meetings, and with each music sitting, my confidence grew in Viju. I'd decided not to use done-to-death romantic hook phrases like 'ishq hua', 'pyaar hua', etc. and thought that there should be some poetry that would make the song sound like an item number while also containing some newness. But the question still remained—what to write?

Next thing I know, the words that came to my mind were absolutely fresh and exciting. I wrote:

Kisi disco mein jaayein,
Kisi hotel mein khaayein,
Koi dekh le na hamein yahan,
Kahin ghoom ke aayein hum.
Chalo ishq ladaayein, chalo ishq ladaayein,
chalo ishq ladaayein sanam.

Viju loved these lines very much and started composing the song with his heart and soul. When he presented to me the composition, I knew that this was going to create history. Viju now wanted David to hear it, but I warned him, 'If David does not understand a song in the music room, then he dumps it. So my opinion is to complete it and then you present it to David as a final song.'

Viju completed the track as per my advice and called in a singer and dubbed the song. One day, I took David along with me to hear the song. Although I'd spoken quite highly about Viju, David still appeared very nervous. 'I have no idea what exactly I'm going to hear today,' David spoke frankly.

We were welcomed into the studio premises with delicious Gujarati snacks and then finally we arrived at the studio and started the music sitting. 'Sir, before listening to the song, I want you to hear the groove first,' Viju told David.

As soon as Viju played the track, David looked at me with astonishment. Perhaps, he was hearing what he had not expected from Viju at all. Viju had created a sound from the mouth, which was the highlight of the song. After 5–6 minutes David got up saying, 'I loved the song. Now you guys can plan for its recording and I'll start planning its shoot.'

Alka Yagnik and Udit Narayan were brought in to sing the song, who sang it magnificently. David too shot it wonderfully with Govinda and Raveena Tandon who added magic with their performances. The film as well as its music were declared super hit after its release. 'Kisi Disco Mein Jaaye' was the most successful song of *Bade Miyan Chote Miyan*.

The year 1998 proved to be a very successful year in my life because two of my films which were completely different from each other, *Kuch Kuch Hota Hai* and *Bade Miyan Chote Miyan*, were released at the cinema halls together. Both the films proved to be musical hits at the box office, and I'm glad that both will always be remembered for their amazing songs.

Movie: *Bade Miyan Chote Miyan* |
Lyrics: Sameer | Singers: Alka Yagnik, Udit Narayan |
Music: Viju Shah

∽

19

'Dilbar'

1999

There are few films that don't leave a mark at the box office, but their songs become immortal and are hummed and remembered forever. One such film was the 1999 Sanjay Kapoor and Sushmita Sen starrer *Sirf Tum* with its chartbuster of a song 'Dilbar'. *Sirf Tum* was produced by Boney Kapoor and directed by Agathiyan, the famous director from the Tamil film industry.

All the songs of *Sirf Tum* were penned by me and composed by my favourites Nadeem–Shravan. Not only 'Dilbar' but the entire soundtrack was a smash hit and was the ninth best-selling music album of 1999. Nadeem-Shravan and I had composed the songs of this film very diligently, but in the beginning, I was not interested in doing this film—the reason being the producer of the film, Boney Kapoor.

A few years before *Sirf Tum*, Anu Malik and I were supposed to do a film with Boney Kapoor, but later Boney had fired me and hired Javed Akhtar to write the songs of his film. I respect Javed Sahab a lot and I have no resentment towards him, but Boney's last words to me had annoyed me a lot.

'Sorry Sameer, Javed Sahab is my friend and I couldn't say no to him,' Boney gave me an excuse.

Boney's word 'friend' had irritated me a lot because if Javed Sahab was his friend, who I was? An enemy? Time passed, I kept writing songs and Boney Kapoor kept making films, but we didn't get to work together.

In between, many films of Boney's brother Sanjay Kapoor had flopped. Boney had dared to make one more film with Sanjay as the protagonist and this time he was trying to be very cautious. He was leaving no stone unturned for its success at the box office. But people in the industry were making fun of his decision. I remember someone had made a joke on the announcement of *Sirf Tum*. This is how it went: One day, Boney came to Sanjay Kapoor and said, 'Sanjay, so far all your films have miserably failed at the box office. Now who will take you as a hero to burn his money?' '*Sirf tum* (Only you),' Sanjay politely replied to Boney.

Boney called me to his house one day and asked me to write the songs for his new film. I believe that, with time, some friends become enemies and enemies become friends. Well, I did not hold any grudges against Boney. And so, I went to meet him. I was ready to do his film too, but I was not able to shirk away that incident and the feelings it had brought up in me. Since I was not Boney's 'friend'—according to him—I decided to behave in a formal way, like a 'professional' lyricist, which was not my nature otherwise.

'Boney, let's talk about the money first,' I politely said to him.

'What?' Boney was shocked to hear what I'd said.

'Yes, I would like to know your budget for lyrics in your film.' I was very clear to him.

Boney did not believe his ears because he knew what I was saying was not my style of work. So he tried to gratify me.

'Look brother, my last few films didn't do well at the box office and *Sirf Tum* has no big star cast. I consider you and Nadeem–Shravan as the heroes of my film. I need your support to put together this project,' he said to me graciously.

'I'm always there for you, but I can't compromise on my fees.' I was very straightforward.

I gave him a figure of what I was charging in the market at the time, but it was an unbelievable amount for Boney. Now, let me disclose something here—Boney is the big producer of Bollywood, and big producers never pay big money.

'Brother, I didn't even have half of what you've just quoted in mind.' Boney was shocked.

Boney started bargaining with me about the fees, but I was sure that I would only write for him if I got paid as per my market price.

'Sameer, please understand I'm making a tight budget film,' he threw a stereotypical producer's line.

'Then please take someone else to write for you if you have a small budget for lyrics,' I replied.

He kept bargaining, but I stood firm on what I had quoted. Perhaps he understood the reason for my resentment or changed tone. Finally, he surrendered and agreed to pay me what I was demanding.

In this way, neither did I mention any previous anger nor did I expect any apology from him. But I had registered my resentment through my changed tone, which he understood well. After this meeting, Nadeem-Shravan and I started making music and writing songs. We were asked to make a dance number on a beautiful tune, so I wrote:

Dilbar dilbar, haan dilbar dilbar
Hosh na khabar hai, yeh kaisa asar hai
Hosh na khabar hai, yeh kaisa asar hai
Tumse milne ke baad, dilbar
Tumse milne ke baad, dilbar

During the recording, when Boney heard the hook word, 'dilbar', he rejected the line. 'To me, it is sounding *dinbhar, dinbhar* (all day, all day) instead of dilbar, dilbar,' Boney Kapoor objected.

I was shocked to hear such a remark from a noted producer. Nadeem and Shravan both got furious upon hearing the feedback. 'Sir, to us it is sounding "dilbar, dilbar" only and we don't see any problem in the hook word. But if you don't like the song, then you can leave it,' Nadeem was straightforward.

After many heated debates, Boney finally okayed the lyrics. I fortunately could convince him for the song. After its release, the film bombed miserably at the box office. So, what became of the song Boney was unsure of? Well, it went on to become a cult number in Bollywood. 'Dilbar' was counted as one of the major hit songs of 1999. In 2018, 'Dilbar' was again recreated in the John Abraham starrer *Satyamev Jayate*, which received an amazing response.

I often think that if I had not convinced Boney Kapoor to use the song 'Dilbar' that day, then Hindi cinema would have been deprived of a wonderful song.

Movie: ***Sirf Tum*** | Lyrics: **Sameer** | Singer: **Alka Yagnik** | Music: **Nadeem-Shravan**

20

'Mujhe Raat Din Bas Mujhe Chahti Ho'

1999

One day, I was on a long road journey and I heard a song on the radio. It was a soothing romantic tune. Gauging my excitement, the driver increased the volume. I liked the song very much. I even asked the driver how he liked it; the driver too went on heaping praises for the song. I was already applauding the lyricist who could write such romantic poetry. To find out who had written the song, I thought of talking to the creator of the song. So I called Jatin.

'Brother Jatin, please tell me, who has written the song "Mujhe Raat Din Bas Mujhe Chahti Ho?"' I asked eagerly.

Jatin laughed out loud after listening to me.

'Brother, I haven't cracked a joke. I have just asked a question,' I said with surprise.

'Sir, your question is in itself a joke,' he replied, finally holding his laughter.

'What do you mean?' I didn't understand what he was trying to say.

'Sir, I am talking to the creator of this song,' he said, and chuckled again.

'What? Did *I* write this song?' I asked him in surprise.

'Sir, I suggest you to do less work. If you do more, you will forget your work yourself,' he laughed at me and disconnected the call.

I felt ashamed of forgetting my own work. I tried remembering the producer and director of this film and then everything came back to my mind as if it were a fresh memory.

Sangharsh was released in 1999 and starred Akshay Kumar, Preity Zinta, Ashutosh Rana and Aman Verma in leading roles. The film had some moments that were spine-chilling. It was a psychological thriller directed by debutant Tanuja Chandra and produced by my favourites Mahesh Bhatt and Mukesh Bhatt. It achieved great success at the box office.

The songs of Mahesh Bhatt's films are always remarkable. In this film too, they tried to be different and gave the responsibility of music direction to the duo Jatin–Lalit for the first time, but I remained their first choice. I used to work mostly with Nadeem–Shravan and Anand–Milind before this. Jatin–Lalit had a desire to work with me since both of them were doing great. I, too, was looking for an opportunity to work with them. Mahesh Bhatt's *Sangharsh* had finally fulfilled our desire.

Jatin–Lalit composed a very good tune and asked me to write poetry for it. The composition had touched my heart, so the words that came out of my mouth had actually come straight from the heart. That's why it struck a chord with all the team members when I narrated it:

Mujhe raat din, bas mujhe chaahti ho,
Kaho na kaho mujhko sab kuch pataa hai

Mukesh Bhatt was also a part of the music session. He also praised the song, but got a little sad. Looking at his expression, I asked, 'Did you not like the song, Sir?'

'No, the song is very good,' he responded quickly.

'Then what happened, Sir?' I wanted to know.

Mukesh ji started describing the film industry as a sinking ship and said that we were giving our best like this song, but these were the worst days for music in Bollywood. Producers investing their hard-earned money had to forget about earnings because even the recovery of the invested amount had become nearly impossible. There was no money and the producers were going through the worst patch of their career.

Just then someone said that Javed Akhtar was waiting outside. Since he was not a part of this film, he had not come inside. I respect him a lot and didn't like someone very senior from the industry waiting for us outside the studio, so Mahesh Bhatt's permission, I invited him inside.

Even after Javed Sahab came inside, Mukesh Bhatt continued lamenting about the good days of the industry nearing its end. He said that the technicians had started demanding huge amount of money as their fees and the music directors had started asking exorbitant amounts.

For a while, Javed Sahab listened to all this. But soon he looked at me and said in his peculiar style, 'Sameer ji, do you know, when I was in my mother's womb, I used to often hear the sound of Mukesh ji's voice, saying the same thing, that the worst time for the film industry had come and making films had become difficult.'

Mukesh Bhatt did not expect this from Javed Akhtar.

Javed Akhtar continued, 'But wherever I go, I see prosperity everywhere. Everyone has work. All are very satisfied with their careers. Producers are making films one after the other. I suppose this is the best phase for the actors. I strongly believe that this is the boom of our film industry.'

Everyone sat in pin-drop silence. They did not have any idea on how to react. Next thing I know, Javed Sahab looked at me and delivered the punch line, 'My brother Sameer, Mukesh ji doesn't want to pay the full fee for your excellent work, so he is scaring you by telling that our industry is a sinking ship. You must quote him a big number because he is making a lot of money nowadays.'

Hearing this, we all laughed out loud. Although it was a fun moment for the rest of us, but Mahesh Bhatt did not like it. Even today, whenever I remind this incident to Mukesh ji, we both laugh a lot.

When the film was released, it went on to become a great success at the box office. It was one of the highest grossing movies of the year. Every Farhad, Romeo and Majnu of the country was singing 'Mujhe Raat Din Bas'.

I would like to share an excerpt from a fan mail (originally in Hindi, which I have translated into English to share with you) related to this song that I recently received.

> Dear Sameer ji,
>
> The song 'Mujhe Raat Din Bas Mujhe Chahti Ho', written by you, is a timeless song. This is an extraordinary, melodious, soulful song, which will always tickle lovers.

Such fan mails are my real awards and, I believe, are what will keep me alive for centuries.

Movie: *Sangharsh* | Lyrics: Sameer | Singer: Sonu Nigam | Music: Nadeem–Shravan

Top: Sameer with the esteemed Filmfare Awards trophies awarded to him for *Aashiqui* and *Deewana*

Bottom: Sameer (*second from left*) alongside (*L to R*) music directors Ehsaan, Shankar and Loy while recording songs for the unreleased film *Dus* at Purple Haze Studio in Bandra, Mumbai

Top: Sameer (*second from right*) at a muhurat ceremony alongside (*L to R*) actors Pooja Bhatt, Raveena Tandon, Padmini Kolhapure, film producer Tutu Sharma and music director Anand (of Anand–Milind)

Bottom: (*L to R*) Sameer, film director Rakesh Roshan, music director Rajesh Roshan, and actors Hrithik Roshan, Kangana Ranaut and Vivek Oberoi during the album release for *Krrish 3*

Top: Receiving the Hindi–Urdu Sahitya Award from Vishnu Kant Shastri, the then governor of Uttar Pradesh

Bottom: Presenting his biography, *Away With Words*, to President Pranab Mukherjee at the presidential residence in Delhi. Also present Member of Parliament Zafar Ali Naqvi

Top: With music directors Anand and Milind at a Bollywood function in Mumbai

Centre: At a Mumbai recording studio with director Raj Kanwar (*centre*) and music director Annu Malik (*right*) while working on the songs for *Har Dil Jo Pyar Karega*

Bottom: (L to R) Actor Jeetendra, actress Ameesha Patel, film director Sawan Kumar Tak and Sameer at a song release event

Top: (*L to R*) Actor Rohit Kumar, music director Himesh Reshammiya, actor Kamal Haasan and Sameer at a recording studio in Mumbai

Centre: Sameer (*left*) with music director and singer Bappi Lahiri (*centre*) and an unidentified guest at a function in Mumbai

Bottom: Sameer's fiftieth birthday celebration. In attendance are (*L to R*) singer Sapna Mukherjee, music director Anand (of Anand–Milind), Sameer, wife Anita Pandey, daughters Shuchita and Sanchita, and singer Alka Yagnik.

Top: Music director and singer Himesh Reshammiya with Sameer at a function in Mumbai

Bottom: Sameer (*far left*) attends the muhurat ceremony of an untitled film at a Mumbai hotel, accompanied by (*L to R*) film director Inder Kumar, film producer Ramesh Taurani, director Kuku Kohli, and actors Madhuri Dixit and Rekha.

Top: Sameer (*centre*) with his favourite music directors, Nadeem (*right*) and Shravan (*left*) at the success celebration of the film *Deewana*

Bottom: Music director A.R. Rahman with Sameer at lyricist Javed Akhtar's birthday party at hotel Taj Lands End, Mumbai

Top: Sameer with music director Anandji (of Anandji–Kalyanji) at the Mirchi Awards in Mumbai. In the background are (*L to R*) music directors Anand Raaj Anand, Wajid Ali and Sajid Ali, singer Sunidhi Chauhan and the late film star Firoz Khan.

Centre: (*L to R*) Film director Sawan Kumar Tak (*behind Sameer*), Sameer, music director Pyarelal, an unidentified budding singer, music director Anandji (of Anandji–Kalyanji) and actor Prem Chopra, at a song release event

Bottom: Sameer Anjaan and Shuja Ali, co-authors, collaborating on the ideation of *Lyrics by Sameer*

21

'Main Aai Hoon UP Bihar Lootne'

1999

Imagine a film where the director initially saw no scope of it carrying any songs because of its intense storyline. But that's not what happened. When the film was released, it not only had a couple of songs, one of its songs became so popular that it helped the film gain tremendous success at the box office. The song became the chartbuster of the year and the identity of the film. I'm talking about the feature film *Shool* (1999). The song in question was 'Main Aai Hoon UP Bihar Lootne'.

After the success of *Satya* (1998), filmmaker Ram Gopal Varma wanted to work with his favourite actor Manoj Bajpai again. But there was no script in which he could've cast Manoj in a central role. One day, his assistant E. Srinivas placed a Bihar-based political drama hardbound script in front of him, which he fell in love with instantly. Both of them jointly wrote the screenplay and Anurag Kashyap wrote its dialogues. In this story, Manoj was shown as an honest police inspector who gets entangled with politicians and vows to end crime and corruption in Bihar. Manoj Bajpai and Raveena Tandon were cast in the lead roles, and Ram Gopal Varma gave E. Srinivas the responsibility of direction. Since the story of the film was serious, and Ram Gopal

Varma was known for experimenting with each of his films, it was decided that there would be no songs in the film. But a few days later, the producer and the director thought that there should be a few songs in the film and agreed to keep two in the film. That's how Shankar–Ehsaan–Loy and I were approached.

We started jamming to discuss the music of the film, which materialized very soon in the form of two wonderful songs. Ram Gopal Varma, who we used to lovingly call Ramu, loved the songs. The director and actors too loved the songs. The shooting of the film began with great enthusiasm and was completed as per the schedule. When the final film was seen, everyone realized that though the film looked good, it seemed to be very dry. Everyone suggested that in order to spice up the film, it must have an item song.

One day when I was returning from the town side after a music sitting, I got a call from Shankar who sounded anxious and, honestly, disturbed. 'Sir, now E. Srinivas is demanding for an item song for the film.' He sounded very annoyed over the phone.

'Okay, so what's the problem? We'll do something,' I said to Shankar.

'No, there is no problem. But first, they said that the film will have only one or two songs because the film is serious and pragmatic. And now, an item song is being requested,' said Shankar. This was the time in the Hindi film industry when item songs were considered a part of only masala films.

'Sir, the film is set in Bihar, and you understand the language and culture of UP and Bihar; please write something keeping that in mind,' said Shankar before hanging up.

Since the film was set in Bihar, and the words 'UP' and 'Bihar' are often uttered in the same breath, I started thinking about the song with these two words in mind.

By the time I reached Bandra, I had the mukhda of the desired item song ready with me:

Dil walon ke dil ka qarar lootne
Main ayi hoon UP Bihar lootne

At first, I was very happy and satisfied with these lines. I immediately told Shankar over the phone about the mukhda of the song. He sounded quite happy to hear the hook, but the call got abruptly disconnected. I started to wonder if he did not like the hook line after all.

I had just reached Andheri—it had taken me 45 minutes to reach there from Bandra, where I reside—when I got a call from Shankar. 'Sameer ji, we've composed the hook you gave us. We want you to listen to it,' Shankar said.

He put the phone on speaker and played the song for me to hear. I was stunned. It was a mind-blowing composition. I appreciated their composition, and the three of them praised my writing.

Within two to three days, I wrote the entire song and met the composers at their studio. When we were ready with the song, we called E. Srinivas and Ram Gopal Varma to hear it. They loved the writing as well as the composition.

'This is just the song I needed,' said E. Srinivas, complimenting us.

Since it was not an ordinary Bollywood song, the challenge before us was to get a suitable voice to sing it. Suddenly, I recalled the name of folk singer Sapna Awasthi, who was introduced to Bollywood on my recommendation to sing the folk song 'Banno Teri Ankhiyan' in Dushmani (1995), which was later dialed up as 'Banno Tera Swagger' from *Tanu Weds Manu Returns* (2015). Sapna sang the item song way better than we had expected and Shilpa Shetty immortalized this item song with her dance and style on screen. E. Srinivas shot it amazingly by maintaining the feel of the song.

'Main Ayi Hoon UP Bihar Lootne' was a purely original Bollywood song that people (mis)took as a folk song. It became a chartbuster in 1999, and will always be remembered as one of the most popular item songs in Bollywood. Even today, when this song is played at any party, people start dancing to its tune.

Movie: *Shool* | Lyrics: Sameer |
Singers: Sapna Awasthi, Shankar Mahadevan |
Music: Ehsaan-Shankar-Loy

∽

22

'Nasha Yeh Pyar Ka'

1999

I am proud of the fact that the team of Nadeem–Shravan and Sameer are considered among the most successful teams in cinematic music history. We were young, talented and raring to rock the world. Every tune we composed became immortal. But an unfortunate accident shattered our team and only thereafter did the world get to know each one of us by our full names. Nadeem Akhtar Saifi. Shravan Kumar Rathod. Sameer Anjaan. In 1999, I was pleased to collaborate with Sanjeev–Darshan, sons of Shravan Rathod of Nadeem–Shravan fame.

After the murder of music magnate Gulshan Kumar, Nadeem shifted to London, whereas Shravan stayed in Mumbai. Subsequently, the magical team of Nadeem–Shravan didn't survive. Indra Kumar started working with other music directors after that, but I was lucky to be still a part of all his films. At the time of making *Mann* (1999), he called Shravan and asked him to compose music for him. Shravan got emotional and refused to work without his partner Nadeem. Shravan suggested to Indra ji that his sons Sanjeev–Darshan were looking for work as music directors, requesting Indra ji to consider them for the job. Both had (they still do) an excellent understanding of music and were ready to compose independently.

Producer Ashok Thakeria and director Indra Kumar met Sanjeev–Darshan to test their music abilities and found both of them capable. The makers decided to launch the young music directors.

Indra Kumar was the director of *Dil* (1990), my first super hit film. Since then, we had had a great understanding and respect for each other. He called me to pen the lyrics for his new film. I loved the premise of the film, as well as the star cast. My favourite and an old-time friend Aamir Khan was part of the film, along with Manisha Koirala and Anil Kapoor. Rani Mukerji was also in it to give a special appearance. I was impatient to know from him who was going to compose the music.

'Sameer ji, we're launching Sanjeev–Darshan as music directors,' Indra ji informed me.

'What are you saying, Indra ji?' I couldn't believe it.

Indra told me about the two young and talented music directors. It was a very emotional moment for me because I had written so many memorable songs for Sanjeev–Darshan's father Shravan Rathod. Indra and I recalled many touching moments working with the awesome-twosome of Nadeem and Shravan. Working with Sanjeev–Darshan felt special because I had seen them since their childhood and loved them like my own children. I used to work with their father Shravan, and with this film, I was getting the privilege of working with his children.

Sanjeev–Darshan were not the only ones who had to prove themselves in this film. After giving so many hit songs and receiving multiple awards, I too saw this film as a challenge. I wanted to prove that I could still write something fresh and romantic.

We started our music sessions. Initially, the duo composer was quite hesitant to debate with me, but I asked them to be relaxed and to not think twice before disagreeing with me. They both were well trained. They were third generation musicians. Their grandfather, Pandit Chaturbhuj Rathod, was an avid promoter of classical as well as semi-classical music. Singers Vinod Rathod and Roop Kumar Rathod were their paternal uncles.

Sanjeev–Darshan worked hard and made a very fresh composition for the audience. With this amazing soundtrack, I was sure of the dawn of two new composers on the horizon. Being the most senior, Indra ji used to interfere a lot. But without offending the director, both young boys deftly finished composing fabulous tunes.

One day, Indra ji called me for a music session. 'Sameer ji, write something with the word '*nasha*' on this tune,' Indra demanded.

Song 'Pehla Nasha, Pehla Khumaar' of *Jo Jeeta Wahi Sikander* (1992) was very popular in those days. Not only Indra, every producer of that time wanted a song with 'nasha' as the hook. Indra's demand was justified as the song was to be shot on Aamir. Now the problem was what to write. I heard the tune a couple of times and abruptly started humming a few words. Everyone wanted to hear me out but I refused.

'Let me polish my words, I'll get back tomorrow,' I told them humbly.

I came back home with the hook word and the tune in my mind. Next day, when I visited them, I had the song in my head. Sanjeev–Darshan adjusted the lyrics over the composition:

Nasha yeh pyaar ka nasha hai,
Yeh meri baat yaaron maano,
Nashe mein yaar doob jao,
Raho na hosh mein deewano.

Both, Sanjeev and Darshan hugged me with immense joy. 'Sir, you made our song,' Sanjeev had tears in his eyes.

'Sameer ji, this is amazing,' Indra ji complimented me on the lyrics.

I thanked the music directors for motivating me. Udit Narayan was called in to sing , and he did justice to the lyrics. Sanjeev–Darshan presented the songs to their father to get his feedback and blessings. Shravan loved the song and blessed them for great success.

Indra ji shot the song beautifully on Aamir and Manisha. Both actors' performances and chemistry were appreciated. This song became the most popular song of the film and the soundtrack went on to become one of the biggest hits of the year.

After the appreciation I received from all over, I breathed a sigh of relief, realizing that I could still write romantic songs. I thanked God for blessing me with success once again. This was the beginning of the second musical innings of my career. I suddenly became the first choice among the young music directors to write lyrics for them.

At times, producers request to write lyrics with words like 'pardesi', 'dhadkan', 'mann', 'nasha', 'dil', etc., and believe this will ensure the success of the song. I think that this simply is an illusion. A song doesn't get success due to any single hook word. There are so many other factors at play. But mostly, it is talent that delivers success.

Movie: *Mann* | Lyrics: Sameer |
Singer: Udit Narayan | Music: Sanjeev–Darshan

∽

23

'Dulhe Ka Sehra'

2000

I have written hundreds of songs that have been super hits and people still love to hum them. In this book, I have not mentioned more than one song from a single film that I've worked on, but I would like to break that rule for *Dhadkan* (2000) and specifically for the songs 'Dulhe Ka Sehra' and 'Tum Dil Ki Dhadkan Mein'. I feel delighted sharing my memories of the birth of these songs with you, but let us take it one at a time.

'Dulhe Ka Sehra' is a very important song in many ways. First, this song has been sung by my all-time favourite Sufi singer, (Late) Ustad Nusrat Fateh Ali Khan Sahab. And the second reason for its importance is its subject. In Bollywood, we frequently make songs for Holi, Diwali, Eid, New Year, Independence Day, and for many other occasions, so that people can play these songs at the corresponding event. There have also been many wedding and *vidai* songs composed in Hindi cinema, but, fortunately, among those songs, my song 'Dulhe Ka Sehra' has achieved a cult status and is played at most weddings by Hindi-speaking people in India and across the globe.

The songs of the movie *Dhadkan* were composed by Nadeem–Shravan and all the songs were written by me in a span of three years. 'Dil Ne Yeh Kaha Hai Dil Se', 'Tum Dil Ki Dhadkan Mein', 'Na Na Karte Pyar', 'Aksar Iss Dunia Mein' and 'Dulhe Ka Sehra' were all super successful songs.

When we were working on the music of the film, we learnt that Ustad Nusrat Fateh Ali Khan was in India at the time. The three of us decided to use the opportunity and meet him at a film party in Mumbai. Nusrat Sahab met us with great love.

'Ustad, I'm your biggest fan,' I said while hugging him.

'And I am a big fan of Nadeem–Shravan and you,' he said, praising our work.

'*Shukriya*,' we replied in chorus.

'I would love to sing for you guys if you've any compositions for me,' he added. This motivated us a lot.

Soon after, the three of us were in London to record 'Tum Dil Ki Dadhkan Mein'. There in London, one day, we got a chance to attend a wedding. During the vidai ceremony, a few words came to my mind. I requested a waiter to get me something to write on, and he came back with few tissue papers. I wrote the entire song at that party. On returning to the hotel, I narrated the song to Nadeem–Shravan, who were extremely impressed by it. The very next day, they made a fantastic composition for the song.

'Which singer should we ask to sing this song? Shravan asked me.

'Nusrat Sahab,' I replied back instantaneously.

Both loved my suggestion.

On returning to India, we were overjoyed to know that fortunately Nusrat Sahab was still in the country. The three of us took an appointment and met him at a five-star hotel. Nusrat Sahab was very happy to hear the composition and agreed to sing the song.

'This wedding song will prove to be my achievement of

this visit to Bombay,' he said while complimenting us.

Everything was finalized. The director of the film, Dharmesh Darshan, was very happy to know that Nusrat Sahab was going to sing for his film and he considered it an asset. The song was to be recorded at Versova in Sunny Deol's recording studio, Sunny Super Sound, on a newly bought 100 channel recording station. When Nusrat Sahab reached the studio, he was happy to see the British sound engineer who used to record him often in London and was now in India at the behest of Sunny Deol.

Nusrat Sahab first inspected the studio, then called Dharmesh Darshan and asked him, 'How are you planning to shoot this song?'

'On one side, the wedding would be going on, while a team of qawwals would be singing this song,' Dharmesh explained the visuals he was planning to shoot.

'Brother, put a *takht* [a long bench or bed] for me, put the mic in front of it, then I will sing this song,' Nusrat Sahab shared his request with Nadeem in the form of a fraternal demand.

Nusrat Sahab, with a dholak player, memorized the lyrics in a corner of the studio until the takht was arranged. The recording started after all preparations were made in accordance with his request, and the final take of this wonderful song took place at seven in the morning.

During the recording, we felt that it was not going to be possible to complete the song that day. As soon as Nusrat Sahab would sing the mukhda, his throat would choke with emotion and he would stop singing, have some water and then ask the engineer to resume the recording. This kept happening for several hours.

When this happened again and again, Nadeem went to the recording booth and said to him, 'Nusrat Sahab, if you have any problem, we can record it some other day.'

'Don't worry. I am afraid that if this song is not recorded today, it will never be completed,' Nusrat Sahab replied to Nadeem.

'What's the issue?' Nadeem wanted to know.

'When I sing "*Main teri bahon ke jhoole main pali babul*", my throat gets choked with emotions on remembering my daughters,' the maestro explained.

Finally, Nusrat Sahab could record the song after 20 retakes. After the recording, he hugged us, said goodbye and left for his hotel. Next day, he flew back to America and passed away after 15 days of singing this song. Alas! We had been hoping to shoot the song on him after his return from the USA.

I am afraid that if this song is not recorded today, it will never be completed. We all cried remembering his words.

Dharmesh shot this song on Kader Khan, giving him the getup of a qawwal. What was happening with Nusrat Sahab at the recording happened with the actors too during the shoot. Akshay Kumar, Shilpa Shetty and Kiran Kumar couldn't hold back their tears on the same lines.

On its release, 'Dulhe Ka Sehra' became the wedding song of the era.

Movie: *Dhadkan* | Lyrics: Sameer | Singer: Ustad Nusrat Fateh Ali Khan | Music: Nadeem–Sharavan

24

'Tum Dil Ki Dhadkan Mein'

2000

D*il, jigar, nazar, dhadkan*—such words had become a part of my life and always proved lucky for me. Sometimes, it was the title of my film, and sometimes it was the hook word of a song. *Dhadkan* (2000) was one of the most successful films of my life. A multi-starrer film with Akshay Kumar, Shilpa Shetty, Mahima Chaudhary and Sunil Shetty, it was produced by Ratan Jain and directed by Dharmesh Darshan.

After making *Raja Hindustani* (1996), a super hit musical film in 1996, Dharmesh Darshan directed the feature film *Mela* (2000) with Aamir Khan, in which he launched Aamir's younger brother Faisal Khan, which miserably failed at the box office. One of the biggest reasons for the film's failure was its casting. *Mela* was said to be a safe formula film—typical Bollywood—but it proved all the formulae wrong, and the film's producers suffered heavy losses.

When a film flops, it is not just the loss of money but the credibility of all the actors and technicians associated with the film also falls; people start questioning you. Their confidence in you drastically drops and they get more cautious in working with you again. So, to bounce back, one has to work harder than before, and that takes time and energy. The same thing happened with Dharmesh Darshan; it took him four years to return to Bollywood. But this time, he made a comeback with a subject of which he was considered to be an expert. After the success of *Raja Hindustani*, he came to be known as the master of romance.

Dharmesh wanted to repeat the hit combination of his previous release *Raja Hindustani*—the very talented troika of that era, which was Nadeem–Shravan and Sameer. At the pre-production stage, Dharmesh called us and narrated the story. It was a love triangle in which the meet-cute, romance, jealousy, breakup, sacrifice, union—all sorts of colours of life—could be shown. I liked the story very much and congratulated Dharmesh for working on such a strong script. We started jamming and discussing the music of the film.

The music tracks we had composed initially were coming out very well, and we were all very excited to write and compose the rest of the songs. The first song we composed was 'Dil Ne Yeh Kaha Hai Dil Se', which later turned out to be a legendary love track. The second song was 'Dulhe Ka Sehra'. Sung by Ustad Nusrat Fateh Ali Khan Sahab, it had a qawwali touch.

Except for a few things, all seemed to be going in the right direction. It was time for the casting of this film. It seemed to us that Dharmesh was going to make the same mistake that he had done in *Mela* while casting Faisal Khan; this time, it was Sunil Shetty. Sunil was a big star at the time, but his image was only of an action hero. Although one of his big films *Hera Pheri* (2000) was also scheduled to be released, but in that film, he was trying comedy. An action star in a hard-core romantic role seemed off to all the well-wishers of Dharmesh.

The next song we were making was to be the title song of our film. The first line came to my mind easily: '*Tum dil ki dhadkan mein rehte ho.'* The line pleased Nadeem Bhai immensely. If he ever got high-quality poetry, he would go to the ends of the earth to find it a perfect composition. This line had touched his heart, and he composed a great tune for it and recorded it with Naresh Sharma, Surinder Sodhi, and a few others, as they were the best instrumentalists of the time.

Akshay Kumar and Sunil Shetty were the heroes in the film. Udit Narayan and Kumar Sanu, both Nadeem–Shravan's favourite singers, were singing for Akshay. Someone suggested that a third voice should be preferred for Sunil Shetty. But most of us felt that it was a bad idea, since these two singers understood Nadeem–Shravan's compositions best and sang them properly.

Regardless, Nadeem Bhai thought of giving Abhijeet a chance. Abhijeet had been pursuing him for a long time anyway for an opportunity to sing a Nadeem–Shravan composition. He called Abhijeet and rehearsed the song with him. 'I want singers who are able to retain my essence in the songs they sing for me,' Nadeem briefed Abhijeet.

'Sir, you give me a chance. I assure you that I will live up to your expectations.' Abhijeet was confident in his abilities.

And then, when Abhijeet sang this song, it reached another level altogether. He made the composition come alive. When it was released, it saw the kind of success that we could have never foreseen. All the songs were super hit, but 'Tum Dil Ki Dadkan Mein' became the most popular. The *Dhadkan* album was listed at the second position in the yearly music charts and became a big hit among the masses. According to the Indian trade website Box Office India, around 4,500,000 albums were sold.

It was clear that people's perceptions can get changed with time. Dharmesh Darshan's flawless direction and Sunil Shetty's acting skills gave an action star the image of a romantic hero, and this could happen due to their hard work. All our fears proved to be wrong, as both Sunil's acting and Abhijeet's singing were loved by the audience. Dharmesh Darshan's conviction proved to be right. I learnt that we should never judge someone too soon.

Movie: *Dhadkan*| Lyrics: Sameer |
Singers: Abhijeet, Alka Yagnik |
Music: Nadeem–Shravan

∽

25

'Iss Pyaar Ko Main Kya Naam Doon'

2001

Mujhe Kuch Kehna Hai was a musical romantic film released in 2001 and was a sleeper hit at the box office. The film marked the debut of Tusshar Kapoor, who was paired opposite Kareena Kapoor, and was directed by Satish Kaushik and produced by Vashu Bhagnani.

It was a time in my career where I had established a known partnership with Anu Malik with many memorable films that we had done together, such as *Biwi No. 1, Soldier*, etc. The music of these films had struck a chord with the audience. When the public likes your work, you enjoy working even more.

When we were offered this film, we thought that it would be wonderful to work on it because we had a very good relationship with most of the cast and crew. My friendship with the director of this film, Satish Kaushik, went all the way back to the time of my second film, *Ab Aayega Mazaa* (1984). Vashu ji and Kareena Kapoor too were very cordial with us. Working for this film was as much fun as working in a home production.

One day, Satish ji called us to his office and narrated the story of the film. He asked us to start working immediately.

This was the period when Anu Malik used to go out of Mumbai to a hotel or resort for music sittings, preferring to work far away from all the worries and hassle of Mumbai. Not only Anu Malik, this was becoming a trend among many of my filmmaker friends, like Abbas–Mastan, Indra Kumar, and many others. It actually was a wonderful idea to go away from the city to somewhere quieter where one could concentrate and focus on their work and deliver their best effort.

Since we did not have much time to go far away from Mumbai, Vashu ji booked a resort in Mud-Island—a beautiful island in Mumbai—and we all reached there on the said date. We were all very excited, as this was the launch vehicle of beloved legendary actor and 'Jumping Jack of Bollywood' Jeetendra ji's son Tusshar, along with it being a big film for a young and emerging star like Kareena Kapoor. We started discussing the music, and I kept writing lyrics while listening to everyone's inputs.

But the hurdle came in the form of a song that Satish Kaushik had planned a big shoot on. Despite the detailed briefing that I had received, I was still blank even after giving it a lot of thought for days.

The situation in the film was such that an average Joe falls in love with a very beautiful girl but does not know how to express his emotions to her. The same dilemma, confusion, shyness of the boy was supposed to be shown in the song. I wrote a lot of mukhdas, but—what do I say about others—even *I* did not like my own writing.

'Satish ji, what should the lines talk about?' I asked him because he was the screenwriter and scriptwriter of the film as well. The subject therefore would have been clearer to him.

'Brother, I think that when there is nothing clear in the boy's mind, then we should focus on his confusion and write something around that,' Satish replied.

I sensed that I was very close to the hook line of the mukhda, so I took the pen in my hand and gestated at him to keep talking about the situation.

'See, the boy has no idea, *ki woh iss pyar ko kya naam de.*' Satish ji took me closer to the line.

I quickly wrote the line I had been blessed with that moment, all thanks to Satish ji.

'*Iss pyar ko main kya naam doon*', I read out the hook line of the song.

The line was appreciated by everyone present because it had effectively translated the core emotion into words.

Often, the hook line of a song comes from the title of the film, or a dialogue in the film jumps out to you during a discussion. During narration and sittings, I always keep my ears open for the correct word or phrase and pick it up from wherever it's possible to seek inspiration. Anand Bakshi, when writing the song 'Zindagi Har Qadam Ek Nayi Jang Hai', took inspiration from the film's dialogue written by Javed Akhtar.

The hook line of the song was final, but now the challenge before me was what should be written next which would clarify and complement the first line. Anu Malik started humming the hook line and made the tune in only a few minutes, which helped me think further.

'*Bechain dil ko kaise araam doon*', I spoke the second line.

On hearing the line, Satish ji jumped with joy and hugged me. 'Bhai, I got my song!' He was all praise was beaming.

Anu Malik was ready with an amazing composition and that too in just a couple of days. The remarkable playback singer Sonu Nigam mesmerized all of us at the recording studio with his soulful voice. Jeetendra ji and his entire family were very happy with the music we had made, and therefore, to celebrate the music release of the film, he threw a grand party at his bungalow.

'Sameer, Anu, you're the real heroes of this film!' Jeetendra ji's compliment was like a blessing for me, for I had idolized him since I was a child.

On its release, the film was a sleeper hit. Tusshar, Kareena and Satish Kaushik were appreciated for their acting and direction. The song 'Iss Pyar Ko Main Kya Naam Doon' was a chartbuster, and the album's sale was recorded as one of the year's biggest. Anu Malik was nominated for many awards for the album. The hook line of this song was liked by the people so much so that it later went on to became the name of a popular TV show.

Movie: *Mujhe Kuch Kehna Hai* | Lyrics: Sameer | Singer: Sonu Nigam | Music: Anu Malik

26

'Zara Zara Behekta Hai'

2001

I have told you the amazing stories behind the super hit songs from many of my hit films. But it will be unfair to my young fans if I do not talk about one of my super hit songs in a super flop film. The song 'Zara Zara Behekta Hai' from the film *Rehnaa Hai Terre Dil Mein* (2001) has developed a cult following amongst young audiences, and is very popular even today.

Released in 2001, *Rehnaa Hai Terre Dil Mein* was produced by Vashu Bhagnani and directed by the Tamil film director Gautam Menon. It starred R. Madhavan, Dia Mirza and Saif Ali Khan in pivotal roles. An official remake of Tamil hit film *Minnale* (2001), *RHTDM,* as it came to be abbreviated and commonly called amongst youth, marked the debut of Dia Mirza and the Bollywood debut of South star R. Madhavan.

One day, Vashu ji called me to his office and requested me to come to Chennai to write the songs for his under-production film. At that point in time, most of my collaborations, following the unfortunate split between Nadeem–Shravan, were with Anand–Milind, with whom I had started to give many hits. It was largely understood that we worked exclusively with each other. So this request from Vashu ji took me by surprise.

'Sir, what are you saying, Anand–Milind will kill me if

they hear that I am going out of Mumbai,' I replied to Vashu ji nervously.

'Sameer ji, please do something. My film will get stuck otherwise.' Vashu ji was eager with his requests.

'Why don't you call the director and music director to Mumbai?' I suggested to him, which would solve a lot of problems.

'Not possible! These South people are very uncomfortable outside their city,' he replied. His response made the nature of creative process very apparent. I thought to myself that creative people, myself included, are very comfortable in their confines to be able to stay in their element. Any change tends to hamper their creative flow, irrespective of the language they speak or the work they do.

Having written innumerable songs in so many of Vashu ji's films and sharing a great relationship with him, I felt terrible saying no to him even after his repeated requests.

'Vashu ji, I can make it work if I go to Chennai in the early morning and come back to Mumbai late at night. But this means I will only be able to give one day,' I requested him to adjust, and he agreed.

I took a day off from my Mumbai colleagues and left for Chennai the next day by an early morning flight. After exactly two and half hours, Vashu ji and I were in a hotel room sitting with Gautam Menon, the director of the film.

Gautam greeted me in Hindi, which surprised me. '*Are waah*, you speak really good Hindi,' I smiled at him. It was good to have someone around who spoke your native tongue. If he would've stuck to English, then there would have been some problem in interacting with him because we had to write a song in Hindi.

Gautam played the recording of the tune on an audio cassette player, and I attentively heard all the compositions.

After that, Gautam started relating the situations of the songs, and I started penning those lyrics. We'd started this session at around ten in the morning and had all the lyrics completed by four in the evening. Meanwhile, tea, food and snacks continued to be brought in for us, so that we did not have to stop working. All throughout the day, I had, running in mind's background, the late-night flight that I had to catch at any cost to reach Mumbai—I was supposed to meet Anand–Milind at 8.00 a.m. next day.

'Zara Zara' took most of my time in Chennai that day because this was a very lengthy tune and had to be a continuous love saga of a girl. In the song, a girl relates her love story in a seamless narrative. It was very difficult for me to write the romantic expressions of the girl, her feelings and the cravings of her heart in a sequence. I kept listening to the director and the tune, and finished the song at 4.00 p.m. on the dot and handed over the pages with the lyrics on it to Vashu ji.

'Wonderful! Nobody could have done this other than you, Sameer ji!' Vashu ji beamed with joy.

'Who is going to sing this song? I want to meet the singer?' I asked Gautam.

'Sir, we've thought of Bombay Jayashri,' he replied.

I was surprised to hear the name of the singer. I was told that since she used to live in Bombay earlier, she is called as 'Bombay Jayashri'. I chuckled to myself thinking that I should have been called 'Banaras Sameer' according to this logic.

I met Jayashri in the evening at the hotel and found her to be a very nice girl. She was a trained classical singer. I wanted her to read the lyrics in front of me, so that I could check her Hindi diction. She was perfect with her Hindi.

'Sir, Jayashri is going to sing it wonderfully!' said Gautam. Jayashri blushed upon hearing her praise from the director of the film.

Then I went to meet the music director of the film, Harris Jayaraj, at his recording studio. He greeted me with great respect. I congratulated him for his brilliant compositions and then left for the airport.

The shoot of the film went on very smoothly. The actors had acted very well, and, most of all, the songs had come out great. But all praises specially highlighted the song 'Zara Zara'.

The music company was very excited about the music of the film and, to promote the songs, requested Vashu Bhagnani to push the release of the film by a month. But he did not listen to them and released the film on the pre-decided date.

On the fifth day of the release, the film was pulled off from the cinema screens. But by then, the song 'Zara Zara' had gone on to become a rage amongst youth. Every FM radio channel was playing 'Zara Zara' on listener's choice back to back. As a response, the public naturally went to the cinema halls to watch the film, which had this soulful romantic song. But unfortunately, the film was removed from the theatres by then.

Vashu Bhagnani realized his mistake and suffered heavy losses.

The film *Rehnaa Hai Terre Dil Mein* failed miserably at the box office, but the song 'Zara Zara Behekta Hai' was loved by the youth as one of the most seductive female Hindi songs of cinema—ever.

Today, When 'Zara Zara' suddenly plays on the radio out of nowhere, young girls and boys not only sing along to it, but smile at the memory of having heard it for the first time long back. And that's the magic of music and of this song in particular.

Recently, I went to an FM radio station where I was told that 'Zara Zara' is one of the most-played songs on FM radio channels. I thank Vashu ji for showing trust in me and giving me the opportunity to write something so beautiful.

Movie: *Rehnaa Hai Terre Dil Mein* | Lyrics: Sameer | Singer: Bombay Jayashri | Music: Harris Jayaraj

27

'Kabhi Khushi Kabhie Gham'

2001

Iconic filmmaker Karan Johar's *Kabhi Khushi Kabhie Gham* (2001), also called *K3G,* was indeed a monumental saga of love and family bonding. It featured Amitabh Bachchan, Jaya Bachchan, Shah Rukh Khan, Kajol, Hrithik Roshan and Kareena Kapoor. The songs of *K3G* are still fresh in our memory even today, the most memorable being its title song.

After the success of *Kuch Kuch Hota Hai,* Karan Johar wanted to make a film with an eternal shelf life. This time too he was very confident in his script and therefore he could easily manage to cast the biggest stars of the industry.

One day, Karan called me to narrate the script, which absolutely blew me away. This was probably the biggest and most challenging film of my career because Karan wanted me to write a title song with an *aarti* or devotional song like temperament. Not only this, he wanted to use it in a variety of moments in the film, such as those of love, happiness, sadness, family bonding, family separation and them reuniting.

After hearing his demands for the song, I laughed and asked, 'Karan, you seem to be very ambitious and demanding this time, don't you?'

'Yes, I am, sir. But I'm sure that you'll fulfill all my demands and will definitely help me make my most ambitious film by penning absolutely fresh lyrics,' he replied with a sparkle in his eyes.

I met music directors Jatin–Lalit and discussed the song. We decided to begin the music sessions, but we were clueless about where to start. So that I could get some cue from the director, I decided to call Karan Johar.

'Karan, who do you think should sing our song?' I asked with inquisitiveness.

'Lata ji.' Karan was very sure about the singer. Eager to know the status of his project, he asked me, 'Sir, are you through with the lyrics?'

'Karan, I haven't started yet,' I laughed while replying and hung up the phone.

This call was very important for me because I wanted to know who he was planning to have onboard to sing this 'reverential' title song. Now, we had a cue—we could start thinking about the song keeping Lata ji in mind. I shared this information with Jatin–Lalit too and asked them to give me a tune to write the lyrics on.

Jatin–Lalit started working on the tunes and presented each one to Karan who kept rejecting them one by one. He had even given us a reference song from the 1986 Bollywood classic *Ankush*—'Itni Shakti Hamein Dena Data'. We all were quite disappointed with our progress, as even working day and night for more than three months was proving to be unfruitful. While we were doing our best in our own capacities, Karan too was discussing the song with a few of his industry friends and well-wishers.

One day, Karan went to meet the film director and his mentor Aditya Chopra. He had been an assistant director and actor in his Bollywood classic *Dilwale Dulhania Le Jayenge* (1995). In that meeting, Karan shared with Aditya Chopra that the title song of his upcoming movie was not working out the way he had wanted it to.

After hearing about the situation, Aditya Chopra closed his eyes for some time and started humming a tune. Karan was astonished by his guru's musical wisdom, who had naturally inherited the art from his father, the great film maker Yash Chopra ji. Tears started rolling down Karan's eyes, and thus, the title song of Dharma Production's *Kabhi Khushi Kabhie Gham* was born at YRF Studio.

Karan Johar rang Jatin–Lalit and me up for a quick music session at his office. He passed us the same tune that he got from Aditya Chopra. The tune was indeed very touching and soulful. After working on the tune for a week, we had the song in place. I wrote the lyrics keeping in mind the title of the film. Karan got emotional and hugged me when I presented the lyrics to him.

'Sir, thank you so much for giving me the song that I can imagine being played in every Indian's house,' said an overjoyed Karan.

Karan went on to shoot the song at mesmerizing locations throughout India and abroad with the biggest star cast of the time. When the soundtrack was released, it sold copies by the millions. The music of *K3G* was a big hit, but the title song topped the charts. I've written innumerable title songs so far, but *K3G*'s title song will always remain special and close to my heart.

Lata Mangeshkar sang the track and made it even more soulful and emotional. The nightingale of Bollywood at 72 sounded as good as she was at her peak. The song pierced right through our hearts and souls. Jaya Bachchan, Amitabh Bachchan and Shah Rukh Khan performed it superbly well on screen.

I still remember that moment from the film premiere

when I saw the audience wiping their tears when the mother senses the return of her eldest son. That's when the first note of 'Kabhi Khushi Kabhie Gham', in Lata ji's voice, reverberates through the hall. It was an exceptional on-screen magical moment created by Karan Johar by capturing a mother's love and intuition in just a few shots.

Even years later after writing the lyrics, I still experience a sense of immense pleasure and satisfaction whenever I hear the song 'Kabhi Khushi Kabhie Gham' play unexpectedly around me, like it happened recently one early morning in Lucknow. It sounded to me exactly like an aarti being played, infusing divinity in the entire atmosphere Karan Johar is indeed one of our industry's gems who had seen the future of the song even before it was born.

Movie: *Kabhi Khushi Kabhie Gham* | Lyrics: Sameer | Singer: Lata Mangeshkar | Music: Jatin-Lalit

28

'Aapke Pyaar Mein Hum'

2002

One morning in 2001, Mahesh Bhatt asked me to see him in his office. I wanted to know the agenda of the meeting over the phone.

'Let's meet and discuss,' Mahesh Bhatt said to me and disconnected the call. When I reached his office, he welcomed me very warmly by holding my shoulders tightly and said, 'Sameer, I want you to go mad again.'

After the murder of music mogul Gulshan Kumar in 1997, the most successful musical combination of that time, Nadeem–Shravan, Sameer, Mahesh Bhatt and Mukesh Bhatt had split up—unfortunately for Indian music. Gulshan Kumar's death was indeed painful for us, but there was a lot of bitterness among the people of the film industry. As time passed, slowly the bitterness subsided and Bollywood returned to its original glory.

'I'm starting work on a movie,' Mahesh Bhatt said to me warmly.

This certainly was good news not only for me but also for Bollywood.

'Congratulations, Mahesh ji!' I happily commended him and asked, 'Mahesh ji, who are our music directors?' I eagerly wanted to know who was I going to be working with.

'Nadeem–Shravan! Who else I can think about?'

Mahesh ji shocked me. At that time, no one in the industry wanted to work with Nadeem or, should I say, they were too afraid to be associated with him. This courage could have only been shown by a man like Mahesh ji—a man with a bold and clear image.

This moment was very emotional for me. After being separated from the music directors with whom I had done the best work of my career, this news brought me to tears. Once again, we were going to work together, and the credit had to go to Mahesh Bhatt.

'Sameer! Where are you lost?' These words of Mahesh ji brought me back to reality.

'Is this truly possible, Mahesh ji?' I wanted to be sure.

'Of course it is! That's why I want you to go mad, I want your madness of *Aashiqui*, *Dil Hai Ke Manta Nahi*, *Saathi* and *Ham Hai Rahi Pyar Ke*,' he said excitedly.

Mahesh Bhatt wanted to prove himself again. He wanted me to get into the mood of the '90s. But at the same time, the film industry had moved on and had evolved, and, with it, the music had evolved too. And then there was Nadeem, who had not worked in the industry for five years. Could we, with the same magic and the same mastery, showcase the art of winning the hearts of the audience once again?

Many questions were echoing in my mind. It was a big challenge. There were some technical problems as well. But, if a director like Mahesh Bhatt had decided to bring us together, then he must have thought this through.

'How will we do this? Nadeem Bhai is in England, and Shravan and I are here in India,' I asked him.

'I know it's not easy, but I will do this film with you guys.' His words relieved me.

The director of this film was going to be Vikram Bhatt,

but the responsibility of the entire project was on Mahesh ji's shoulders. He was doing his best to put the film together.

Mahesh ji delivered this happy news by calling Nadeem in London, who was struggling with a huge personal crisis at that time. But he listened to him and gladly accepted his offer. 'Bhaijaan, your wish is my command. I will do this project with the promise that our magic will work on the public once again.' He sounded very confident.

The pre-production process had started in full swing. Mahesh ji called Shravan and me to his office and put Nadeem on speaker. It was a formal script narration for all of us. This was going to be a romantic horror film. We realized that there was a lot of musical scope in it and started discussing the music over the phone.

Soon after, Mahesh Bhatt, Shravan and I, along with a musician, were on our way to London to do a music sitting with Nadeem. He came to pick us up at the London airport. We all met Nadeem with great warmth, but what stood out was Nadeem and Shravan holding each other tightly for a long time. It was an emotional moment.

In London, we started composing the music and writing lyrics. One day, Mahesh ji surprised us by telling us that while his brother Vikram Bhatt was directing this film, he would be directing a song in it. He explained the vision he had for the song: a young woman playing violin in the jungle, a handsome man walking towards her, and eventually getting seduced by her. I wondered why the woman was playing a violin in the jungle, but if Mahesh Bhatt was saying so then surely there would have been some solid reasoning.

Nadeem–Shravan came up with a very melodious tune. And then I wrote the following lines over it:

Aap ke pyaar mein hum savarne lage,
Dekh ke aap ko hum nikharne lage,
Is kadar aap se hum ko mohabbat hui,
Is kadar aap se hum ko mohabbat hui,
Toot ke baazuon mein bikharne lage.

Maheshi ji loved what I had written, 'I knew that I was never going to regret taking the three of you together. I'm proud of you all!' It was a big compliment from him.

Mahesh ji shot the song amazingly well. The moments were captured just the way he had told us. The film was a super hit. It was the second-highest-grossing film of the year, only behind the Shah Rukh Khan, Madhuri Dixit and Aishwarya Rai starrer *Devdas* (2002).

The album was a chartbuster in 2002 with songs that became very popular. The songs got international acclaim and was even appreciated by Paul McCartney of the Beatles fame. 'Aapke Pyaar Mein Hum' became a rage soon after its release and was played at almost all weddings and celebrations for several wedding seasons.

Movie: *Raaz* | Lyrics: Sameer | Singer: Alka Yagnik | Music: Nadeem-Shravan

29

'Mera Rang De Basanti Chola'

2002

Working with the music legend whom some of our industry friends call Bal Bhagwan, another name for Lord Krishna, was an experience of a lifetime. How do I begin to talk about it! He is the one and only A.R. Rahman. *The Legend of Bhagat Singh* (2002) was based on the life of the celebrated freedom fighter, with Ajay Devgn playing the titular character. It was directed by Rajkumar Santoshi and produced by Ramesh Taurani.

Unfortunately, in the same year, there were many films on Shaheed Bhagat Singh, which is why this film couldn't get the response it should've got at the box office. Although, *The Legend of Bhagat Singh* did fetch Ajay Devgn a National Award for his brilliant acting.

'Sameer, penning lyrics for this film will be a challenge for you because you've been writing for romantic films only,' said Rajkumar Santoshi to me.

I had written many films for Rajkumar Santoshi in the past and had a great rapport with him.

'Santoshi Sahab! Yes it's true, but here instead of praising the beauty of the heroine, I'll be writing for my motherland, so for me it is a similar task,' I replied back.

Actually, there were two 'legends' that were the reasons

behind why I wanted to do this film. First, it was the subject of the legendary freedom fighter Shaheed Bhagat Singh whose bravery and love for the country I had admired since my childhood, and the second was the opportunity to work alongside the living legend and Oscar winner A.R. Rahman, who I was going to work with for the first time. I was extremely enthusiastic about meeting Rahman. Working with him would allow me to observe him from a close distance, and I was very eager to know how he was going to treat the subject.

'For the music sitting with Rahman, we've to go to Chennai,' said Ramesh Taurani over the phone. Well, what had to be done, had to be done. Next thing we know, there we were—Rajkumar Santoshi, Ramesh Taurani and I—flying to Chennai.

In Chennai, we were staying at one of the Taj hotels. Ajay Devgn was supposed to join us the next day. Although he was not needed, Rajkumar Santoshi wanted him to be present, just so that he could get the feel of the subject and the era depicted in the film.

We were waiting to start the music sitting in the evening, when Santoshi Sahab's phone rang. It was A.R. Rahman's manager. 'Rahman Sir will start the music sitting at 12.30 a.m. with you all,' informed the manager.

Although, we had known that Rahman Sahab works in the night, this was surprising for all of us, as, in Mumbai, we would always do these meetings during the day.

At around 11.30 p.m, we were informed that Rahman would now see us by 2.30 a.m. It was a little too much for us to digest, and it enraged me a bit too.

'By 2.30 a.m, we would be wide awake having completed our sleep,' I said sarcastically.

Rajkumar Santoshi laughed at my comment, but Ramesh

Taurani calmed me down. We started chatting about music legends of the past era, and that's how we passed our time until the time of the meeting. The manager again rang up Santoshi Sahab.

'Santoshi Sahab, now he is going to say that Rahman Sir will meet by 4.00 a.m.,' I commented

With fingers crossed, Santoshi Sahab picked up the call.

'Sir, you can now proceed for the sitting,' said the manager.

'But, where exactly do we have to come?' Rajkumar Santoshi asked anxiously.

'You will be informed once you reach at the gate of the hotel,' said the manager, and the call was disconnected.

We all proceeded towards the gate. The manager called again and asked us to follow a black car. 'That car will take you to the place where Rahman Sir is waiting for you.'

This was an experience of a lifetime. Following the black car, I couldn't stop myself from chuckling and saying, 'It looks like we're working on a Bond film.' Everyone laughed with me.

It was absolutely dark outside. After travelling for about an hour and a half, after having crossed a very famous hotel, the car finally stopped at the seashore. The whole journey was quite dramatic and mysterious. We saw a man standing on a narrow path leading towards the ocean, holding a lantern in his hand.

The driver got out of the car and said to us like a character from a murder mystery, 'Sir, please follow this guy. He will take you to Rahman Sir.'

We, like prisoners, followed the instructions of the driver and started walking behind the strange lantern-wielding man.

'I take my words back. It's not a Bond film; it is definitely a horror film,' I said.

Ramesh ji almost fell on the ground laughing upon hearing my comment. After walking for about 200 yards between thick foliage, we reached an open space facing the sea. The lantern man pointed towards a hut made of dry grass next to a shrine of some Sufi saint and asked us to go there.

As we entered the hut, we found A.R. Rahman and an attendant who was there for serving tea and water. Rahman Sahab got up from his place and just uttered a few barely audible words to us. 'Hello, how are you?' he must have asked.

Next, he went back to his spot and wore his headphones. We kept staring at him patiently for some time, watching him enjoy whatever he was listening to with closed eyes. Ramesh Taurani looked at Rajkumar Santoshi and me with great surprise.

What is all this? Ramesh Taurani gesticulated at us.

Santoshi Sahab motioned to us to be patient.

After some time, Rahman gave the headphones to the director Rajkumar Santoshi to hear seven musical tunes and note the one that he liked the most. Santoshi Sahab heard all the tunes and wrote his remarks about the tune he liked. The headphones were then passed to the producer and then to me. We all heard the tunes and told Rahman which tune we found the best.

Rahman got up from his place, shook hands with us and asked us to go back to the hotel. As we reached the hotel, Rahman mailed the final tune to us.

It was 6.00 a.m. when I received his email. I immediately sat down to writing the lyrics, and within an hour, I had the most beautiful song of the film with me— 'Mera Rang De Basanti Chola'.

Next night at around 2.00 a.m., when we went for the recording at his studio, we couldn't believe our eyes. In front of us was Udit Narayan sleeping on a swing. On a couch lay Subhash Ghai. Ram Gopal Varma was sleeping on a staircase. We got to know that 'Rahman Sahab is dubbing Asha Bhosle'.

He dubbed our song by around 4.00 a.m. with Sonu Nigam on a click track, which was again a shock for us. We were confused as to what our song would finally sound like. Actually, A.R. Rahman records all music instruments and voices separately. And it is only when he sits with all the tracks on his computer, the magic of A.R. Rahman truly begins.

After five days of hardship, surpises, mysteries and dealing with the unknown, when we finally heard the song, we all had tears in our eyes and smiles on our faces. We knew why Rahman is a great musical maverick. All the suffering—if I may call it that—turned out to be worth the result we had with us.

Movie: *The Legend of Bhagat Singh* | Lyrics: Sameer | Singer: Sonu Nigam | Music: A.R. Rahman

∽

30

'Tere Naam Humne Kiya Hai'

2003

Let's talk about one of the hit songs of 2003. It was the title song of the film *Tere Naam* (2003). The soundtrack of the film contained 12 songs, out of which there were three different versions of 'Tere Naam'.

Starring Salman Khan and Bhumika Chawla, *Tere Naam* was a remake of the 1999 released super hit Tamil film *Sethu*. Directed by Satish Kaushik, it was produced by Sunil Manchanda and Suresh Talreja. But to make this film, the producers had to knock at the doors of many film stars.

On one hand, no big star wanted to do it because of the tragic ending of the story, and on the other hand, they weren't refusing it due to the box office success of the original Tamil film. In the beginning, the film was offered to Aamir Khan. He liked the story but asked for one year's time. Next, the film went to Shah Rukh Khan, who liked it as well but asked for time to prepare for the character. The producers could not wait, so they kept contacting other film stars; they even offered it to Sanjay Kapoor, but the proposal did not work out. After a year, when the producers approached Salman Khan, he immediately said yes. It was that time when Salman had reportedly broken up with Aishwarya Rai and probably therefore could relate to the story. After this, the production of the film started with full swing.

At the time of music production, the director of the film and my old friend Satish Kaushik called me. During the conversation, he specified to me the name of the music director he wanted to work with.

'I want Himesh Reshammiya to compose the songs of my film,' Satish Kaushik said.

'This is your film and you have every right to choose who you want to work with, but I cannot work with Himesh,' I replied.

'Why? Have you had any bad experience with him?' He was curious to know.

'No.'

'Then what happened?' He wanted a clear answer from me.

'The kind of personality he has and the kind of attitude he carries, I don't think our association will survive. And most importantly, I don't want to see your very ambitious film suffer because of any possible conflict.' I put my point very clearly in front of him and left for my house.

But Satish kept chasing me to write the songs. I was adamant that I wouldn't do this film. I even went to London around the same time to write for *Raaz* (2002) with my favourite Nadeem–Shravan. But Satish was not ready to give up.

Satish tried his best to get a yes from me. He would call me during my London stay, but I was determined that I was not going to work with Himesh at any cost. The more pressure Satish put on me, the surer I became that I would not say yes. I had created a very bad image of Himesh in my mind, due to which I was not willing to work with him. I have often had creative differences with my music directors, but have never fought with anyone. But I was sure that Himesh's temperament would not match mine and that I would definitely get into a fight with him. And for this fear, I was running away from him. But then, who can run away from destiny? And finally, what happened was always destined to happen.

'Dear Sameer, if you will not write the songs of my film, then I too will leave this film as a director.' One morning, I received this message from Satish and it changed my mind completely. I was being emotionally blackmailed by Satish to write the songs. I finally said yes because I never wanted to be the reason for someone's career failures.

Satish was so happy to have me onboard. First of all, he asked me to write a *bhajan*. I sent him the lyrics of the bhajan from London, which was needed for the *muhurat* ceremony of the film. On my return from the UK, Satish arranged for a music sitting, where Himesh and I were called. I was surprised to find a completely different Himesh from that of my imagination. He greeted me humbly and appeared as a nice person. He was also a talented and creatively equipped music director. His modest attitude destroyed my presumptions about him, and thus we connected instantly.

We started jamming and discussing the music for the film. Himesh wanted a title song from me and it was to be made in three different versions. I wrote the lyrics of the title song: '*Tere naam humne kiya hai jeevan apna sara sanam.*' Himesh and Satish both loved the lyrics and approved it. Soon, Himesh composed a sonorous music track full of Indian melodies. Himesh kept his eye on each detail while making the songs, which impressed me a lot.

Till that time, songs used to get recorded with a full orchestra. Sunny Super Sound studio was booked for the pupose. Musical instruments were recorded live. The atmosphere at the recording studio reminded me of the era of the 1990s. Udit Narayan and Alka Yagnik were called to sing the title song. They both added their magic to the songs with their blessed voices, which was soon going to surprise and fascinate listeners. Everyone was very happy with the end results. This song had set the mood for other songs of the film.

After the release of the music, all songs of *Tere Naam* became huge hits, and the biggest hit of the album was the title track. The film was equally successful at the box office. It was appreciated for Salman Khan's new look and amazing performance, and Satish Kaushik's flawless direction.

I often think that I could have never given such wonderful songs to my fans if I had not worked with Himesh on *Tere Naam*. After the success of the film, producers started demanding Himesh and me to come together in other projects. Both of us complied to the request and made many more amazing songs.

This film taught me a lesson: I promised myself that, in the future, I would never make any assumptions about anyone without knowing him or her well.

Movie: *Tere Naam* | Lyrics: **Sameer** | Singers: **Alka Yagnik, Udit Narayan** | Music: **Himesh Reshammiya**

∽

31

'Main Yahan Tu Wahan'

2003

The duo of B.R. Chopra and Dilip Kumar, after giving many hit movies, like *Naya Daur* (1957), *Mazdoor* (1983) and *Dastaan* (1972) wanted to come again in the 1990s in Chopra's most ambitious family film *Baghban* (2003). Dilip Kumar, the veteran actor, had heard and loved the script, but this project could never take off with him in the lead role due to the declining health of the thespian, and the script of the film remained in cold storage for a long time.

This project was very close to B.R. Chopra's heart, and he was sure that if this film was made, it would be highly appreciated. So, he didn't stop and continued discussing it with other film stars, but nothing worked out.

Meanwhile, in the year 2000, Amitabh Bachchan had been looking very graceful playing old characters on screen. One day, B.R. Chopra spotted him in the movie *Mohabbatein* (2000) on TV, and his eyes started to sparkle.

'Call Amit over for a meal one of these days. I want to meet him.' The veteran producer–director asked his son Ravi Chopra.

Amit ji used to respect B.R. Chopra very much. So, he came to meet him as soon as he got the invitation.

B.R. Chopra spoke his mind to him. He narrated the

storyline of the film with great enthusiasm, 'If a man helps his children to walk their first steps in life, why can't they help him walk his last steps.'

Amit ji was very impressed by hearing the one-line pitch and realized that Chopra's instincts were right about this project. Therefore, he gladly accepted his invitation to be a part of the film.

B.R. Chopra was 88 years old at that time, and looking at his health, he handed over the responsibility to direct the film to his son Ravi Chopra. However, Ravi, being not only the senior Chopra's son but also his assistant director, thought that if his father were to direct this project, it would reach new heights. At last *Baghban* took off with Amitabh Bachchan and Hema Malini as the lead pair, and Ravi Chopra as the director.

Music director Uttam Kumar and Hasan Kamal were chosen to write and compose the sound tracks. The songs they produced were presented to Amit ji who said that the songs sounded ancient. He was of the opinion that music in the year 2000 should reflect the time. Therefore, a new team was formed and the responsibility was given to Aadesh Shrivastava and Javed Akhtar. After the first music sitting, Javed Akhtar refused to write the songs by saying that he couldn't do a film where the youngest team member was 70 years old.

It's not to be forgotten that, in the beginning of the twenty-first century, the responsibility of filmmaking in Bollywood was completely left to the younger people, and having grey hair meant retirement. It was funny that Javed Sahab, who said this, was also considered among the elders of the industry at that time. I respect Javed Sahab very much who apart from his great writing skills is also known in the film world for his spontaneity and frankness. Perhaps, this was his own style of saying no to this project.

After Javed Sahab's refusal, I was called to write the songs.

It was an honour for me to work with Bollywood veterans like B.R. Chopra and Ravi Chopra. I loved the story and had no objection to working with the grey-haired elderly team members as well.

Aadesh and I started making the songs. Everyone was very happy with the output and we were enthusiastically engaged in our work. Amit ji too had been enjoying all the songs. When all of a sudden, one day, news came that B.R Chopra's wife had passed away. This would have indeed been very painful for an 88-year-old man whose long-time life partner had suddenly left him forever. After that misfortune, everything stopped for some time.

But gradually, we resumed work on the music. Aadesh had composed a very emotional tune. While I was listening to the track, B.R. Chopra's brief echoed in my ears. The storyline showed an elderly man calling his wife from a telephone booth and asking her about her well-being. I wrote the lyrics and next day went to present it to B.R. Chopra.

'Papa ji, Sameer ji has come to narrate the lyrics to you,' Ravi Chopra told his father.

'*Okay, sunao puttar ji.*' He was instantly ready to take the narration.

I began, '*Main yahan, tu wahan...*'

After hearing the first line, he didn't react much.

I repeated that line once again. '*Main yahan, tu wahan…*'

The expression of his big eyes spoke slightly louder this time, and I knew that he had grasped at the words. It felt very fulfilling to see this great filmmaker react to my words, so I repeated that line yet again: '*Main yahan, tu wahan…*'

He now closed his eyes, but it was clear from his expressions that his attention was towards my words.

Now, I read the second line: '*Zindagi hai kahan.*'

He raised one hand towards me, gesturing me to stop,

and started crying. Panicked, I turned to Ravi Chopra, who also motioned to me to stop. I understood that my words must've reminded him of his wife. After a while, he looked at me affectionately.

'Puttar ji, like me, your words are going to touch the heart of every listener. God bless you,' B.R. Chopra patted my back to encourage me.

I touched his feet and took his blessings. For me, this appreciation was no less than the National Award.

Once out into the world, everyone loved the song. Amitabh Bachchan, accompanied by Alka Yagnik, sang it beautifully. I applaud Aadesh Shrivastava for making Amit ji sound so wonderful in the song. On screen, both Hema Malini and Amitabh Bachchan brought the song to life.

Baghban turned out to be one of the most heart-touching movies to have come out of Bollywood. The film's soundtrack was one of the year's highest-selling. One can truly feel the pathos in this film. We witnessed people crying at the premier of the film.

B.R. Chopra's meaningful and intimate story, Aadesh Shrivastava's catchy music, Barun Mukherjee's photography, Anchala Nagar's remarkable writing and Ravi Chopra's brilliant direction were the highlights of the film. I was lucky to contribute to this beautiful film through my poetry.

The great twentieth-century filmmaker B.R. Chopra made a very successful film in the beginning of the twenty-first century, and proved that no matter how old gold is, it will remain gold.

Movie: *Baghban* | Lyrics: **Sameer** | Singers: **Amitabh Bachchan, Alka Yagnik** | Music: **Aadesh Shrivastava**

32

'Dhoom Machale'

2004

I vividly remember walking into YRF Studio, or the Yash Raj Film Studio, following a call from them. I was a bit surprised since everything about the project had been kept under wraps, and I had virtually no clue about it. Yet, I was very excited, since it is always a matter of prestige to work for a banner like Yash Raj Films.

I went to the reception and informed them of my presence. A call was made and, within seconds, I was ushered to a large meeting room. Completely unaware of what was to follow, I opened the door only to see the dynamic Aditya Chopra get up from his chair and greet me very warmly.

As he did so, I realized that there were a bevy of people sitting in the room. Some known and some unknown. I could instantly recognize Aditya's younger brother Uday, model turned actor John Abraham and, of course, megastar Amitabh Bachchan's talented son, Abhishek, sitting in the room. But there were two more people who I had never interacted with earlier. Aditya probably noticed my confusion.

'Sameer ji, please meet Sanjay Gadhvi, the director of our new film, and Pritam, the movie's music director. They have worked with us earlier on *Mere Yaar Ki Shaadi Hai* [2002].'

I exchanged pleasantries with all of them and sat down for

the briefing session. That session was an eye-opener in many ways. Aditya informed us that he had been observing the youth for a long time and they seemed to be having a lot of zest and passion for biking. He further added that there were in fact biker gangs that were operating in different cities across the country as well. And he wanted to capture this essence in a relatively small budget film with a young star cast, fast paced action and some really groovy music.

The movie was to be called *Dhoom*, and we were to meet again for the first sitting of the title track.

I knew I had my job cut out for me!

But I got a call sooner than I expected. Sanjay, the director, had called me up and sounded worried. I arrived at the studio to see two dejected faces staring at me—Sanjay and Pritam!

'What happened?' I asked.

'We created a very catchy tune,' Pritam said.

'Okay. Play it for me,' I replied.

'Can I sing it out?' Pritam asked.

'But how? You don't have the lyrics with you!' I replied.

'Yes, we used dummy lyrics for the moment,' Sanjay butted in and I asked Pritam to proceed.

I heard the tune, which all of you today know as the signature tune of the *Dhoom* series. At that time, it went: 'Main teri hoon, main teri laila!'

Needless to say, I was hooked and felt it had potential. And then it suddenly struck me—why were they sad?

'Adi Sir rejected the song!' The response came.

I found it strange, but I also knew that if Aditya had rejected it, there must be a reason behind it. And so I went to his cabin to enquire about the reason behind him rejecting the song.

'Sameer ji, I don't think the lyrics work. The word "laila" sounds too dated, almost from the eighties and must've been used in more than 300 movies. As I had said, we need to have a fresh outlook in this movie.'

I heard Adi out and left the studio while still humming the tune. For some reason, I did not want to give up on it. I sat in my vehicle and my mind started buzzing with ideas. Then it hit me. I thought if a movie titled *Dhoom* would succeed at the box office, what would the newspaper headlines read like? Surely something like '*Dhoom ne box office pe machayi DHOOM*!'

At that very moment, I hummed 'Dhoom machale, dhoom machale dhoom' instead of 'Main teri hoon, main teri laila'. I had hit the nail on the head. I knew I had struck gold, and I wasn't mistaken. I asked the driver to turn the vehicle back to the studio and I rushed straight into Adi's cabin.

Before he could ask me anything, I sang the lines out to him. Adi got up from his chair, walked up to me and then, all of a sudden, hugged me tightly. The compliments he gave me that day are still etched in my memory. He was amazed that the title 'Dhoom' was in front of everyone, right from Sanjay to Pritam to himself, yet it was I who was able to so seamlessly infuse the titular word into the song.

Once that was done, fitting '*Ishq ishq karna hai karle...*' seemed like a piece of cake in comparison. And the rest, as they say, is history.

But nobody knew that we would be returning for a second and third instalment of the series as well. And so popular was the phrase I had coined that Aditya said that for *Dhoom 2*, the entire song was to be in English, but the catch phrase of 'dhoom machale' was to remain as it is.

For *Dhoom 3*, it was a new challenge altogether, since Hindi and English versions had already been attempted and we were obviously not going to try out Chinese or Japanese versions of the same. So, Adi came up to me and told me that I had to completely alienate myself from the thought process with which I had written the earlier Dhoom songs and pen this song afresh. Like always, I was up for a good challenge, and thankfully, I didn't disappoint Aditya and the audience this time either.

But the point I want to drive home is that an average listener hears a song in five minutes and enjoys it or rejects it, never realizing that, like magic, it was created out of thin air or nothingness. And how surreal it is that, if the catch phrase '*dhoom machale*' had never come to me on that drive home back from Aditya Chopra's office, the composition of one of India's biggest blockbuster hits—if not the biggest—in the twenty-first century, would have never existed!

Movie: ***Dhoom*** | Lyrics: **Sameer**
| Singer: **Sunidhi Chauhan** | Music: **Pritam**

33

'Aashiq Banaya Aapne'

2005

Aashiq Banaya Aapne was a 2005 romantic thriller film starring Emraan Hashmi, Sonu Sood and Tanushree Dutta. The film marked not only the debut of former Miss India Tanushree Dutta as a leading actress but also Aditya Dutt as director and Himesh Reshammiya as singer. The film got the latter a Filmfare award for the highly catchy title track in the 'Best Playback Singer' category. The film will always be remembered for its melodious songs.

Himesh Reshammiya was a big name in the industry for his melodious pop compositions and was also known for the experimentation in his projects. As a debut director, Aditya Dutt was curious to know from Himesh who he was planning to bring on as the film's lyricist.

Himesh replied, 'Let us bring the romantic and title song warrior Sameer ji to pen our songs.'

Himesh invited me to dinner and asked me to write for his upcoming film. The year 2005 was a very busy year for me; I had 27 films to write songs for, so I wanted to excuse myself from this. But Himesh insisted that I pen at least one song.

Meanwhile, a young boy joined us for dinner.

'Sir, he is our director, Aditya Datt.' Himesh introduced Aditya.

Aditya was a well-brought-up guy. He greeted me and joined us for dinner, and more importantly for the discussion about the film.

'What is the title of the film?' I asked Himesh.

'Sir, the title is *Aashiq Banaya Aapne*,' Himesh replied to my question.

Hearing the name of the film, I got anxious about what would happen if they asked me to write the title song.

It was as if he had read my mind. 'Sir, I would request you to write the title song of my film,' Aditya asked me politely.

'*Beta*, you will have to excuse me from this.' I was sure that I was not going to write this title song.

'Why, sir?' Both Himesh and Aditya unanimously expressed their shock at my response.

'Because Anand Bakhshi ji has already written a cult song using that line. Since I'm sure I can't write anything bigger than him, you will have to excuse me,' I replied.

'Sir, Nana ji had written a different song,' retorted Aditya immediately.

Nanaji? Aditya had left me puzzled.

It was then that Himesh told me that Aditya was the great lyricist Anand Bakhshi ji's grandson. I was confused even further. *Why is he not asking his grandfather to write lyrics of his first film*, I thought to myself. According to me, this could have been the best tribute from him to his grandfather. I felt sorry for the young generation who try to distance themselves from the legends of the industry.

Although, the food that night was delicious, the conversation over dinner had left me in confusion and dilemma.

'Please give me some time to think about it.' I excused myself and left the hotel.

I got busy with other projects and forgot about the meeting I had had with Himesh and Aditya. One day, Himesh came to meet me at my place and insisted that I hear a track he had made. It was a great retro-style melodious pop composition. I was surprised and never expected it to come from Himesh.

'Wow! This is a sure shot hit composition,' I congratulated him for creating something so fresh.

'Now, quickly dress it up with great lyrics,' Himesh said, in one breath.

'But, what to write on this,' I was puzzled.

'Title song of *Aashiq Banaya Aapne*!' Himesh was so confident that I was not going to refuse his request this time.

I laughed at his confidence and hugged him for his love and respect for me.

I started working on the lyrics, which were ready in a week's time. Soon, we were all set to record it. The title song was sung by Himesh Reshammiya and Shreya Ghoshal. Although Himesh normally speaks without any vocal inflections, he sang the song in a nasal tone. He did a commendable job with his rendition, which was based on Sufi style music. In all honesty, it sounded awkward to me during the recording, but Himesh was confident with his experiment and eventually it did its magic.

It was an absolutely fresh song, nowhere similar to Anand Bakshi's '*Dard-e-dil, dard-e-jigar dil main jagaya aapne… Pehle to main shair tha, aashiq banaya aapne*'. Himesh presented it to many of his friends and asked if this song reminded them of any Bollywood song. No one said that it had any resemblance to any old or classic song.

Aditya Datt shot it beautifully on newcomer Tanushree Dutta and Emraan Hashmi, and both of them performed wonderfully on screen. The chemistry between the actors was palpable, and the film went on to become one of the biggest hits of the year.

One day, Himesh told me that Aditya Datt had dedicated

the title track to his grandfather. He even told me that Anand Bakhshi ji loved the song and wished us good luck. At an event when I met Aditya, I hugged him and said sorry to him for not understanding his point of view earlier. I was so happy with Himesh and him that I decided to write all the songs of the film.

'Sir, I always wanted to gift a hit song to my grandfather,' said an emotional Aditya.

After winning the Filmfare Award in the 'Best Music Director' category for *Tere Naam* in 2003, Himesh was back with a bang with *Aashiq Banaya Aapne*, for which he won the Filmfare Award for Best Playback Singer and was nominated for Best Music Director.

Audiences had welcomed with open arms the freshness of the prolific Sufi western fusion sound of *Aashiq Banaya Aapne*. The music was on top of the charts from day one, and remained so in the hearts of the listeners for a long time.

Movie: ***Aashiq Banaya Aapne*** | Lyrics: **Sameer** |
Singer: **Himesh Reshammiya** |
Music: **Himesh Reshammiya**

34

'Jhalak Dikhla Ja'

2006

In 2006, a film titled *Aksar* was released. It was known for its songs, the biggest of which was 'Jhalak Dikhla Ja'. This was one of the biggest songs of music director Himesh Reshammiya's and my career.

Aksar was directed by Anant Mahadevan and produced by Narendra and Shyam Bajaj. The film featured Emraan Hashmi, Udita Goswami and Dino Morea in lead roles. This was my second film with Himesh after the musical super hit film *Tere Naam* (2003). There was lot of pressure on both us to come together in a project to recreate our 'magic'. There had been so many offers earlier, but we finally united again in *Aksar*.

After the success of *Tere Naam* many music directors had followed the melody of Nadeem–Shravan but had failed miserably. People were bored listening to the very same old compositions of the 1990s and therefore many films bombed at the box office. A bad workman always blames his tools. Super talented Himesh Reshammiya was not going to curse the evolving taste of the people; he changed himself according to the time and moved on. He had already started the new trend of Sufi and rock fusion with *Aashiq Banaya Aapne* (2005). *Aksar* was one such film whose music belonged to the new trend.

I consider Himesh to be one of the finest gems of our industry; he believes in teamwork. He can discuss each word of the lyrics for hours on a stretch. If someone tries to convince him against any word or line he is fussy about, he thanks them for the suggestion. He has often debated with me on the songs I wrote for him, but always in a healthy and positive manner.

Usually, the music director first makes a tune and gives it to the lyricist to write poetry over it, but something different happened this time. After taking the brief of the film from the director, Himesh and I reached his music room but both of us kept talking about how the music of the film should sound like. As soon as I stepped into his office, three words came out of my mouth—'*Jhalak dikhhla jaa*'. Himesh immediately turned and looked at me.

'What did you just say?' Himesh asked.

'Jhalak dikhla ja', I replied back.

Himesh listened to these words and drowned himself in thinking, like a great scientist gets lost in solving a puzzle. I could sense that he was ruminating on the music of the film, so I requested him to compose the track for the lyrics and left for my house.

One day, when I was in the middle of a meeting, Himesh called me and requested me to meet him that day itself. I assumed that the music track was ready. I got curious to hear it and reached his office after the meeting. He played a very peppy track.

'This is mind blowing, Himesh,' I congratulated him.

'Thank you, sir. Now give me the second line,' he asked me.

I was surprised that he was asking me for the second line when I had not even given him the first line.

'Brother, let me write the first line,' I was confused.

'But you gave it to me that day,' he replied back very casually. He reminded me that I'd given him the first line as 'Jhalak dikhla ja' on the very first day and he'd made the track keeping those words in mind.

'But the music here is very long and those were just three words, so I have to write more words to fit the length of the music.' I could barely hold my laughter, I was so amused and perplexed at the same time.

'Sir, I'm repeating those three magical words four times. I'm done with my first line,' he replied back with a smile.

He immediately played the track and sang those three words four times in four different ways in his trademark nasal sound. I was surprised by his mastery over music. He'd made me his fan.

After some time, I gave him the second line which he loved a lot—'*Ek baar aaja aaja aaja aaja aaja*'. Now, we had the mukhda in place. After a couple of days, I submitted the full lyrics and it was finalized in just one meeting. It was an amazing song and everyone loved it, but nobody predicted that it would become such a huge hit. The song that was made silently with no fuss was about to make noise in the entire world.

As soon as this song was released, it became a hit. This song started being discussed all over the world. Not only me, the whole world had become a fan of Himesh who turned simple words into something extraordinary with his singing. I believe that in this song, singing should be commended more than the poetry. Himesh had reached the pinnacle of success after this song.

According to Box Office India, a trade website, with around 1,500,000 units sold, this film's soundtrack album was the year's eighth highest-selling. The fame of this song did something extremely bizarre. Never in a thousand years could we have imagined that news from different corners of the country would tell us that snakes came out from their hiding-holes on hearing this song. The song was even banned somewhere in Gujarat by the local populace who claimed that the song 'attracted ghosts'. Apparently, people who sang the song said they were felt possessed by spirits and started behaving in a strange way—they reasoned that the lyrics '*aaja aaja*' (literally, 'come come') invited ghosts.

Once, Himesh and I were in Gujarat for a musical show. Himesh had to sing some of his hit songs. But as it turned out, young boys and girls only wanted to groove to this song—on repeat. After having listened to the song for nine to ten times, I thought that they would have gotten tired by then. But to our utter surprise, towards the end, someone in the crowd started shouting 'once more, once more', and they resumed dancing with even more vigour.

Movie: *Aksar* | Lyrics: Sameer | Singer: Himesh Reshammiya | Music: Himesh Reshammiya

35

'Tera Suroor'

2006

Music director Himesh Reshammiya was much in demand among the people after singing exceptionally popular songs like 'Aashiq Banaya Aapne' in 2005 and 'Jhalak Dikhla Jaa' in 2006. He was a different Himesh till *Tere Naam* (2003), but he had changed his style in these two songs. His fans obsessed over his cap, his singing style with his face tilted up and his nasal singing. Every act and move of his was liked and talked by the people, and social media was full of his praises.

In the meantime, the Punjabi and Bhojpuri film industries had started the trend of singers choosing acting as their second profession. The new-found success of reality shows and live concerts had probably given Himesh too an idea that the public was ready to see him as a hero on the big screen. To cash in on this, Himesh Reshammiya finally set his foot into acting in 2007.

Industry rivals and critics were waiting to laugh at Himesh, thinking that they would find the music, singing and acting in the film to be weak. But Himesh silenced everyone, doing his best in all three departments. Not only did the film prove to be a super duper hit, the entire album of the film was well appreciated. But one of its songs surpassed all praises, getting its '*suroor*' over people's minds. It was the sensational song 'Tera Surroor'.

Himesh and one of his friends once talked amongst themselves that that they should make a film with Himesh as the protagonist. But the conversation stopped at the question of who would invest crores of rupees in the production of the film. Consequently, the idea ended then and there. Himesh had given T-series very successful films in the past, which is why he used to share a good relationship with Bhushan Kumar. One day, Himesh opened his heart to Bhushan, talking about his proposal, which Bhushan did not reject entirely.

'Let's first release a music album and see what response it gets from the market. If the album is successful, then T-series will produce your film,' Bhushan promised.

Himesh got excited hearing the plan and decided to work on the album. He gave me a call once he was out of the T-Series office to discuss the album. The chain of action now looked like the following: First, Himesh had to do the title song—if the title song was good, then the other songs would need to be made—if all the songs were good, then the album would be released—and if the album was appreciated, then the film would be made and Himesh's acting career would be launched. I cannot explain the pressure of responsibility and accountability that I had felt for writing the title song. I started working on the song keeping my fingers crossed.

Himesh had wanted an interesting and punchy hook word on which the title song could be mounted. One day, I was reading a poetry book and a poet's name came in front of me—the poet was Suroor Barabankavi. Suroor Sahab was a great Urdu poet. The word '*suroor*' thus got stuck in my mind—suroor, or ecstasy or hangover.

Since the people were already hungover on Himesh's singing, I thought that 'suroor' would be an appropriate hook word. It wasn't even a difficult word that needed to be explained much. It is a poetic word but easy to pronounce and fairly common in usage. I told Himesh that I had got the hook word for the title song.

In the evening, when I met him and shared with him the hook word, he went silent for some time. Actually, he was taking in the word, revelling in it, soaking it up. And then, when he emerged from the trance, he started praising the hook word and said this was also going to be the title of the album.

He got busy in composing the track keeping the word 'suroor' in mind, and I, at the same time, became busy in completing the lyrics. Himesh loved the lines I wrote for him:

Ooooo huzuuuuuuur,
tera tera tera surroor.
Meri baatein, meri yaadein, tanha raatein
tera tera tera surroor.

Himesh composed this song in the same style as his fans' expectations. The album was launched in a big way and was an instant hit. Bhushan Kumar was very happy with the result. T-Series started planning the film on a grand scale.

The film was titled as *Aap Kaa Surroor* (2007) starring Himesh Reshammiya in his debut as an actor, along with Hansika Motwani and Mallika Sherawat. It was a romantic thriller. Sitting on the piano, a long-haired, cap-donning Himesh, singing through his nose, found a place in people's hearts. He played a musician in the film and gave a mind-blowing performance.

Dharmendra, Sunny Deol and Bobby Deol starrer film *Apne* (2007) was released at the same time as this one. Despite this challenge, *Aap Kaa Suroor* did very well at the box office. The film was a hit and the album was counted as one of the best albums of the year.

I have always noticed that Himesh takes good care of all his compositions. Through the beats, he tries his best to sound fresh each time. Another thing he pays great attention to is the hook word. According to him, the hook should be repeated several times because of which the song remains in people's minds and gets them to hum along.

There was also a time when songs were made in a grand style. Those songs were songs of grandeur with heavy musical arrangements, and this trend had been started by the legendry music director A.R. Rahman. But like so many other things, music was also changing with time. Himesh's USP was a simple rhythm. He always loved neat and clean sounds, avoiding heavy sound of any instrument. The mantra of Himesh's success can thus be contracted into a hook line, along with a basic groove of the song, plus a theme-tune that he used to make for each of his songs.

Who knew that the song 'Tera Surroor' would become so popular that the sequel of his debut film was going to be called *Teraa Surroor* (2016).

Movie: *Aap Kaa Suroor* | Lyrics: Sameer |
Singer: Himesh Reshammiya |
Music: Himesh Reshammiya

36

'Crazy Kiya Re'

2006

The *Dhoom* series became a musical rage. Many gave the credit to the title song of the first edition. After the huge success of *Dhoom* (2004), the expectation from *Dhoom 2* (2006) was immense. Producer Aditya Chopra who has a great understanding of music and cinema called me for a music sitting to his Andheri office at the YRF studio.

'Welcome, Sir!' Aditya received me warmly.

'Thank you, Bhai,' I hugged him.

We sat down and started chatting and remembering the 'Dhoom Machale' song and its success. After sometime, music director Pritam joined us.

'Sir, give me yet another rocking dance number like "Dhoom Machale" for *Dhoom 2*,' Aditya requested me.

'I will try my best,' I replied, crossing my fingers.

The three of us sat there discussing for a long time how the songs of *Dhoom 2* would be. This session turned out to be a very constructive one. I could understand what was going on in his mind. After a few months, the title song of the film was composed—'Dhoom Again'—and turned out as an English song. Even after a lot of effort, Hindi wordings could not be added to it, except the signature line of 'Dhoom Machale' from the first Dhoom film. Well, the producer, director and music director of the film were satisfied with the song and we got busy making other songs.

The next song was to be shot on Aishwarya Rai. All the team members were very excited about this. It was to be shot with a large number of dancers on a large set. Aishwarya was a massive star of that time. Her fans were eagerly waiting to see her in this film. She was also waiting to set the screen on fire by dancing in a glamorous avatar. So, dear reader, you can understand the pressure on the music team.

Pritam had composed an unbelievable tune with an Arabic touch to it. The use of the tablas was also well integrated into the track, which was definitely set to be a chartbuster. The tune was to everyone's liking and was approved by Aditya with some changes. Now the producer, director and star, all had their eyes on me.

Pritam sat down with a rapper and embedded the initial part of the song with a Hip Hop rap. English phrases, such as 'she is sexy' and 'sexy lady on the floor', along with the mood of the song was set to take people onto the dance floor.

Just like Majnu was wandering in search of Laila, similarly, I too was drifting mentally in search of the hook line or the signature word of this song. One day, Pritam called me and told me that Aditya Chopra had been calling him every day to ask if 'Sameer ji' had given him the lyrics or not. But I couldn't give him any good news because I still didn't have a great line.

'No problem, sir. Take your time. Something great will come soon yet again.' He encouraged me and hung up the phone.

One day, I wrote something, met Pritam and narrated it to him, but he rejected all my lines by saying 'maza nahi aa raha hai, sir.' I still remember that while writing this song I went through massive stress that I hadn't experienced in my entire professional life. In fact, one day, a friend of mine, on seeing me this restless, ended up jokingly asking me whether bhabhi ji (referring to my wife) had sent me a notice.

But one day, finally, my brain lit up, and I was blessed by my lord with the words that I was looking for: '*Crazy kiya re*!'

I knew that the word 'crazy' was very commonly used by people in an appreciative sense—'he makes me crazy' or 'she was very sexy and made me crazy for her'. I called Pritam and gladly announced that I had got the line and I was coming to the studio to share it with him.

On reaching the studio, I found Pritam standing at the gate waiting for me. He jumped upon hearing the line and bowed down to me, appreciating the hook line we had all been waiting for with bated breaths. We completed the song in a couple of days and went to the YRF studio to present it to Aditya.

After hearing the song, Aditya hugged me.

'Sir, who is the faqeer who blessed you with everlasting youth? I must find him for his blessings,' he commented appreciatively.

I had tears in my eyes.

'How do you know the language of the youth so well?' Aditya was overjoyed.

'I was blessed by a young filmmaker called Yash Chopra ji, who will never grow old till his last breath,' I replied.

On hearing me refer to his father as my inspiration, Aditya got emotional.

I really meant what I had said. According to me, Yash Chopra ji was indeed the youngest old man of Hindi cinema, the greatest film director of romantic tales.

Sunidhi Chauhan sang 'Crazy Kiya Re' flawlessly in a slightly throaty rendition. A huge set was put up at the YRF studio for shooting the song. Director Sajay Gadhvi picturized it astonishingly well on Aishwarya Rai.

'Crazy Kiya Re' became one of the most popular songs of the year.

Not only 'Crazy Kiya Re', but the entire *Dhoom 2* album was made keeping the younger generation in mind, who were later seen (or heard) with the songs playing in ear-piercing volume, blasting from their car audio systems, with the windows rolled down. It also became the favourite dance number at discos and nightclubs in India and across the globe amongst youth.

At the success party of *Dhoom 2,* Aditya congratulated me and encouraged me for *Dhoom 3*.

'Sir, please start looking out for the hook of the *Dhoom 3* title song from now itself,' Aditya laughed.

Each song comes to me with some kind of challenge. Today, I enjoy the success of 'Crazy Kiya Re', but I will never forget how this song had troubled me. *Waqai, iss gane ne mujhe sabse zyada crazy kiya.*

Movie: *Dhoom 2* | Lyrics: Sameer | Singer: Sunidhi Chauhan | Music: Pritam

37

'Hare Krishna Hare Ram'

2007

The story goes that the Amitabh Bachchan starrer film *Don* (1978) had been completed, but the length of the movie was a tad short, so director Chandra Barot decided to add a song. 'Khaike Paan Banaras Wala'—the song in question—turned out to be the engine for the film, which achieved tremendous box office success due to the bonus song added at the last moment. Now is the time to talk about another song that became an engine for the mega success of another film—the Akshay Kumar starrer *Bhool Bhulaiyaa* (2007).

In 2007, the horror comedy psychological thriller Malayalam film, *Manichitrathazhu* (1993) was remade as *Bhool Bhulaiyaa* in Hindi, produced by T-Series and directed by Priyadarshan. The film was also inspired by the Hindi movie *Poonam Ki Raat* (1965). The film was ready to be released, and Priyadarshan was very pleased with the end result. But Bhushan Kumar, the producer, was of the opinion that something was missing in the film. After many previews of the movie, one day while coming out of the theatre, Bhushan looked thoughtful.

'Pritam, we must enhance the film musically,' said Bhushan.

Priyadarshan didn't like the creative interference of the producer.

'Bhushan, our film already has great songs,' replied Priyadarshan.

'But there is no title song in it, and I think we really need one,' retorted Bhushan in an authoritative tone.

Pritam's working style is different from other music directors. Pritam gives you a basic tune to write lyrics on before going into detailing and dressing-up the final song. This working style was new for me because, in the past, I had worked with music directors who either used to give me a ready composition to write lyrics on or they would take my lyrics before and make the composition on it.

It is always a learning experience when you collaborate with different people with their unique styles of working, but I strongly believe that it takes chemistry between two individuals to create history. I am happy to say that Pritam and I always get along really well.

It was a challenge for me to bring the titular phrase '*bhool bhulaiyaa*' in the song. Pritam made a rough track for me to write on, but the appropriate poetry was not coming to me.

After so many sessions I came up with, '*Teri aankhein bhool bhulaiyaa, teri baatein bhool bhulaiyaa*'. However, we were both sure that something was still missing in the song. It sounded flat—not interesting enough to hook listeners to. While penning a song, we keep the director's vision intact, but at the same time we also think why will people like it? How can a song become a chartbuster? In the process of experiment and in search of the USP, we often do some magic and that magic comes from within.

One fine morning, a line randomly came to my mind—'*Hare Krishna Hare Ram*'—and I suggested it to Pritam with a few hesitations. I thought this phrase was still fresh in our memory in reference to Dev Anand's 'Dum Maro Dum', a cult song that will remain in our memories till we die. How could we make this new song sound different from the old 'Hare Krishna Hare Ram'? Although, Pritam loved the idea and assured me that he was going to weave this old phrase into a new, modern and melodious composition.

'Sir, you don't worry! I'll make it an absolutely new song altogether,' said the talented music director.

Pritam's confidence and assurance was quite pleasing to me. He went missing for a long time to work on the song. One day, he presented the track to me, and I was amazed to hear it. His new composition inspired me to write further. I knew it was definitely going to be a chartbuster. We were confident that this was the composition we were looking for.

We confidently presented it to the producer and the director of the film. Priyadarshan was not interested in any new song in the film; he was even reluctant to come to its screening. But when we all heard it together, the air was instantly cleared. The new song was immediately accepted and welcomed into the film.

'The soundtrack is a pleasure to listen to,' said the proud producer Bhushan Kumar.

'The song has a vibrant and lively feel to it. There's also a lot of energy associated with the phrase, "Hare Krishna Hare Ram"' Priyadarshan added with a lot of appreciation.

Interestingly, many things were not part of the film from the beginning—like the song 'Hare Krishna Hare Ram'. Saif Ali Khan was approached for the role of Dr Aditya Srivastava. Abhishek Bachchan was asked to play Shiney Ahuja's role, but he had turned down the offer. Akshay Kumar was not the first choice to play the male lead. Rani Mukerji was offered the role of Avni, which was later played by Vidya Balan. Originally, Aishwarya Rai and Katrina Kaif were the first female choices for *Bhool Bhulaiyaa*. They had turned down the offer due to scheduling conflicts, and were replaced by Vidya

Balan and Ameesha Patel (Vidya Balan had to take Kathak lessons for this film).

Initially, we did not know that that we were going to create something so memorable. 'Hare Krishna Hare Ram' turned out to be a 'sing-along' kind of number. The Hinglish track was pretty different from the usual lot.

'This track is an absolute listener's delight,' said Akshay Kumar, when he heard the song for the first time.

Akshay loved the funkiness of the song and took it on a different level by performing it brilliantly. I must not forget to mention that the costume designer and choreographer too added a lot to the success of the song.

Just after the music release, a court case was filed accusing us of hurting people's religious sentiments, and I was summoned by the court. The honorable High Court judge heard the case and realized that there was nothing wrong in the song, and the case was nullified in the first hearing itself.

The film's soundtrack was one of the year's best-selling albums. 'Hare Krishna Hare Ram' undoubtedly became the engine driving the already stellar film to its much-deserved, great success at the box office.

In 2022, Hindi cinema was going through its worst phase. Films of big stars were flopping one after the other. Due to the impact of the Covid-19 pandemic, people were apprehensive of coming to theatres. At such a time, Karthik Aryan starrer *Bhool Bhulaiyaa 2* was released, which proved to be the biggest blockbuster Hindi movie post-pandemic. Even after 15 years, the magic of 'Hare Krishna Hare Ram' worked once again. This amazing song revamped into a fresh new style became the reason for the super success of the sequel.

I firmly believe that while working on a particular film you don't know the fate of the project, your hard work and commitment pays in the end. I'm sure every great thing one comes across has an inspiring story behind it and is worthy of sharing with the world.

Movie: *Bhool Bhulaiyaa* | Lyrics: Sameer |
Singer: Neeraj Shridhar | Music: Pritam

38

'Jab Se Tere Naina'

2007

Sanjay Leela Bhansali can undoubtedly be called today's Guru Dutt. Every actor who makes his debut in Bollywood wants to collaborate with him. Working with SLB is a dream come true for many. He is not only a great filmmaker but a first-class human being too. He has made several extraordinary films in his lifetime. His films are reflective of his deep personality. Let's talk about his very ambitious romantic film *Saawariya* (2007). This film marked the debut of two star kids, Ranbir Kapoor, the son of actors Rishi Kapoor and Neetu Kapoor, and Sonam Kapoor, the daughter of actor Anil Kapoor and former model Sunita Kapoor.

Many years ago, one day, when I was sitting with Jatin–Lalit at their studio, Sanjay Leela Bhansali walked in. That was my first meeting with him.

'Sameer Sir, This is Sanjay ji. He is making a film called *Khamoshi*.' Lalit introduced me to him.

It was a very brief and casual meeting. SLB came into light after his second film *Hum Dil De Chuke Sanam* (1999), but we never worked together. One day, the famous producer and my old friend Bharat Shah called me.

'Sameer ji, you've got to help me,' Bharat Shah sounded very upset over the phone.

'Tell me, Bharat Bhai, how I can help you?' I asked in assurance.

'See, I'm making a film called *Devdas* and you've got to write a song for it,' he told me.

I met Sanjay Leela Bhansali and wrote a song for him on a situation in the film that was really difficult to write on. The song was called 'Morey Piya'. SLB loved that song, and it went on to become one of the most popular songs of the year. He had promised that we'll again meet soon for his next project. But his next film *Black* (2005) had no musical scope. After three years, I got a call when I was in Hyderabad. SLB's assistant told me that he wanted to meet me.

On my return, I met SLB. He was very courteous. He told me about *Saawariya* and said, 'This is your kind of film.' Salman Khan, Ranbir Kapoor and Sonam Kapoor were going to be featured in it. I met Ranbir and Sonam; they looked beautiful. I was sure that this was going to be a big film. SLB introduced me to the music director of the film, Monty Sharma, who comes from a renowned musical family. He is the nephew of the famous music director Pyare Lal ji.

SLB narrated to me the story of *Saawariya* and he briefed me about the situation of the song I had to write. It was a song about love at first sight. A young boy spots a beautiful girl, and now he is dying to meet her again and romance her. I loved the story and the situation, both but what he said next went over my head.

'Sir, I want this song to be remembered as the "towel song",' SLB said excitedly.

'Meaning?' I was confused.

'I'll be shooting the song with Ranbir wrapped in just one towel and singing the song,' Sanjay was very clear what he was going to do.

Although I couldn't visualize his towel song that time,-

but I was sure that if he was confident about his ideas, then this song was surely going to be remembered for many years.

Monty Sharma had made a soulful, melodious track. Sanjay loved the track because he likes melodiousness. The composition was given to me for lyrics. At home, I tried singing something holding a towel in my hand but nothing worked out. I was in a state of turmoil, completely baffled about what to write.

Subsequently, I tried to recall SLB's brief for me.

'The boy has gone crazy since he saw this gorgeous girl.' The director in my head reminded me of the situation.

I wrote '*Jab se tere naina, mere naino se, laage re*' and smiled. When I shared it with Monty, he loved it too. I completed the song in a short while and went to submit the lyrics to SLB. He simply loved it and approved it without cutting or adding a line to it. He was in shock at how I had managed to complete such a beautiful song in a short span of time.

'"Jab Se Tere Naina" is a beautiful artistic expression of love,' SLB complimented me.

It was Monty's suggestion to SLB that singer Shaan could be tried for this song. Shaan sang it so beautifully, adding soul to it.

'Shaan you made this song "*shaandaar* (majestic)",' I said, after the recording, to which everyone laughed.

One day, I was invited to the shooting of the song. Standing at a distance, I was watching the master director. SLB is indeed a perfectionist. There was a shot where Ranbir had to lie-down laughing and get up and sing the song. He was very particular about what beat actor should catch. SLB appeared to me as a very musical director. After so many re-takes, he approved the shot. Ranbir went through a tough time. But, looking at his dedication, I was sure that not only a remarkable towel song but a star was in the making too.

I witnessed the song gradually getting better and better in each department it touched. The way it was thought, composed, written, choreographed, shot and performed, I was sure that this song was going to be immortal and would be remembered by listeners for a long time to come.

The song turned out to be the biggest hit of the year. I salute Sanjay Leela Bhansali for conceptualizing the towel song and making it a milestone in Hindi cinema. Ranbir made the song come alive and a superstar was born with it.

Movie: *Saawariya* | Lyrics: Sameer |
Singer: Shan | Music: Monty Sharma

39

'Allah Duhai Hai'

2008

Race was an action thriller film directed by Abbas–Mustan and produced by Ramesh Taurani in 2008. The filmmakers would have never imagined that it would achieve such a level of success that it would go on to be converted into a film franchise. After the success of *Race* (2008), they made *Race 2* in 2013 with bigger names than before. *Race 3* was made in 2018 with superstar Salman Khan and an even bigger budget. In all three films, the directors kept changing so many things, but what never changed was the title song 'Allah Duhai Hai'. This song has stayed in the minds of music lovers ever since 2008 through 2018, and who is to say until when in the future.

Film directors Abbas–Mustan are known for their remarkable thriller films as well as for their amazing songs. After *Dhoom* franchise, Pritam and I were very much in demand in Bollywood, and various mainstream filmmakers wanted to collaborate with us. Abbas–Mustan called both of us to write and compose the songs for *Race*. We were signed on by producer Ramesh Taurani. I believe that every film is a challenge and when *Race* came in front of us, it was seen as an even bigger challenge. We happily accepted it and got down to work.

The film had a total of six songs. But we were first asked to make the title song, which was to be a dance number, to be filmed on the film's cast—Anil Kapoor, Akshaye Khanna, Saif Ali Khan, Bipasha Basu, Sameera Reddy and Katrina Kaif. Since the title of the film was *Race*, the hook word of the title song was expected be in the song repeatedly. Now the challenge before me here was how to fit in the English word 'race' in a Hindi song. This was very easy in *Dhoom* because 'dhoom' is a Hindi word. We were confused about how to include the hook word 'race' into a song.

Even after many days of struggle, I could not do much about 'race'.

One day, Pritam, upon seeing me helpless, asked me, 'What happened, Sir? You look very disturbed?'

I just smiled at him, as he was aware of my problem.

'Don't worry. I think I've a solution to our problem,' Pritam said. 'Sir, let's forget the word "race" and make a great dance number.' He looked very excited about his idea.

'But the makers are demanding that the word "race" be made a hook word for the song,' I expressed my concern to him.

'We will figure all that out later. Let's move forward right now,' said Pritam.

Perhaps, he had a point. Pritam delivered a superbly composed track after a few days. After listening to it, I thought that maybe this was going to be our song. I wrote the first two lines on that track:

Allah duhai hai, betabi chaayi hai
Mushkil judai hai, haan tere pyaar mein.

These lyrics were complementing the track very well. Pritam liked my poetry. And on his request, I handed him the entire lyrics in a few days. But I was still clueless about what was to be done with the word 'race'.

So, by now we had a wonderful dance number that had a hook phrase, 'Allah duhai' but no 'race'. I was unaware of what was going on in Pritam's mind.

'Sir, now let's have a couple of lines of the song in Hindi and English mixed. And here you can bring the word "race",' Pritam said to me.

I gave it some thought with a renewed zeal. I thought that the whole world is engaged in a race today—some people are in a race for money, some in a race of fame, while some others are chasing the queen of their dreams. I kept thinking along these lines and I wrote:

Race saanson ki
Race chahat ki
Race dhadkan ki
My heart is racing on.
Nasha tera... Nasha...Nashila nashila hai
Allah duhai hai, betabi chaayi hai

Pritam believes in presenting a complete song to the director rather than just a composition or a part of it. So he wanted to dub the song with the best available singers. He called Sunidhi Chauhan and Neeraj Sridhar to the recording studio the very next day to dub the song. Both the singers sang the song exhuberantly and took it to another level.

The song was now ready to be presented, which the producers and all of us were looking for. It was the perfect dance number with poetry and music, all at its peak.

When we called the directors and producers to the studio to present the song, we couldn't have foreseen they would like this song more than we expected. Abbas–Mustan shot the song in an excellent manner. The dance direction, cinematography and performances of all the actors made this song immortal.

Pritam believes in talent. He seeks the best, irrespective of where it is. He used a guitarist sitting in the USA and another instrumentalist playing from Israel. Like Rahman, Pritam is always in search of the best musical talent and uses them at the right place.

I will give credit for the success of this song to Pritam, who is not only talented but is also gifted with the ability to gauge the talent of others and bring out their best. Hats off to Pritam! How he got me to write this song is an art in itself!

When something is done with conviction, it becomes immortal. The song 'Allah Duhai Hai' has become immortal in Hindi films. I can say it with conviction that even if the filmmakers make a *Race 10* one day, and even if there is nothing in it from the old installments, 'Allah Duhai Hai' will still be in that film.

Movie: *Race* | Lyrics: Sameer | Singers: Neeraj Shridhar, Sunidhi Chauhan | Music: Pritam Chakraborty

40

'Mora Piya Mose Bolat Nahi'

2010

National award winning director Prakash Jha is known for his deeply rooted sociopolitical films. After making a very successful film *Apaharan* in 2005, he took five years putting together his next film on the big screen. His next film *Raajneeti* (2010) was a tangy masala mix of the Mahabharata rustled up with a garnishing of *The Godfather*. It was a multi-starrer film with Ajay Devgn, Ranbir Kapoor, Nana Patekar, Katrina Kaif, Arjun Rampal, Manoj Bajpai and Naseeruddin Shah in lead roles.

Music director Aadesh Shrivastava called me one day and asked, 'Sir, will you write a song for a good film?'

'Aadesh, what's the movie?' I asked.

He refused to tell me the name of the film until I had agreed to write for it.

'Sir, I'm talking about Prakash Jha's next project, *Raajneeti*,' he finally shared the name of the film and the filmmaker only after I had said yes. And from there on, the roller coaster journey started.

I knew about *Raajneeti*. Prakash Jha had shared the information of the film with me long back saying that he was busy converting Mahabharata into a film. I had worked with Jha ji before as well and had a very good working relationship with him. I have always respected him as a brilliant filmmaker and an honest human being. He has great understanding of music. I believe that he uses songs quite skillfully and judiciously in his films.

We met at Aadesh Shrivastava's studio to discuss the film. Now, Aadesh's style of working used to be very different. He knew the art of breaking the ice. He would make sure that the environment in which we all worked was cheerful. He would do so by cracking jokes and sharing funny industry anecdotes before any music sitting. Not only that, he was a very talented music director as well. He never looked worried about the hows and the whats, owing to the belief that good songs could only be made in a relaxed atmosphere. Today, he is not in this world, but I strongly believe that he is always among us through the hundreds of amazing songs he composed in his lifetime.

As always, after a hilarious chit-chat session, Aadesh switched to film discussion. He told me that Prakash Jha had told him that the song was not to be picturized as a lip-synced number in the film, rather it was going to be played in the background. Resentment would be shown between the hero and the heroine in the song. Lastly, Aadesh shared a wish with me that he had been looking forward to make a classical song since a long time.

The track that he composed was an absolutely heartwarming classical tune. I gave him a line: '*Mora piya mose bolat nahi*'. He loved the line and sang it on track, and it fit perfectly. Prakash Jha also loved the line. So, we had the hook line, but now the problem was with the second line. Whatever Iine I would suggested would be rejected by both Aadesh and Prakash Jha. I, too, could not understand what to write because '*Bolat nahi*'s *radeef* was very limited and difficult. Radeef is the last word of every rhyming line in a piece of poetry that is repeated.

After some time, the conversation between us escalated to a fight, and I decided to leave the film. When Prakash Jha heard this, he laughed and said, 'Sameer ji, I don't think *that* is needed.'

Finally after a week, I was blessed with the second line. I wrote, '*Mora piya mose bolat nahi, dwar jiya ke kholat nahi.*' I was very confident this time. When I narrated it to Prakash Jha and Aadesh, they jumped up in joy and said yes to the poetry. After that, I geared up to complete the song with all my energy, and soon finished it and submitted it to the director and music director.

'What is the plan for the song?' Prakash Jha asked Aadesh.

Aadesh told him very enthusiastically that he wanted to treat this song the same way as legendary music directors like Naushad and S.D. Burman used to record their songs. Aadesh wanted to record classical instruments live like it used to be in the old days.

After listening to Aadesh, Prakash Jha took a long pause and said that he had immense respect for the great musicians, but wanted to know why they were not trying something new in the new era. 'We should not forget our younger fans who will be singing the song and keep in mind the choices of today's audience,' Prakash Jha told Aadesh.

Aadesh felt that Prakash Jha's mind had changed and he was now asking him to compose routine Bollywood songs, not a classical one.

'So, are we going to dump the lyrics and replace them with an item?' Aadesh asked.

'No, my brother. But I want you to try something new,' Prakash Jha replied immediately.

'I didn't get you,' Aadesh looked confused and asked Prakash Jha.

'Why can't we try a modern composition on classical poetry?' Prakash tried to make him understand his point of view.

Hearing this, Aadesh Shrivastava went into deep thought.

'And I am only asking you to do this experiment because I am sure you can do it very well,' Prakash Jha praised his music director.

Aadesh composed a beautiful semi-classical 'Mora Piya Mose Bolat Nahi', which turned out to be the best song of the film. On Prakash Jha's request, Aadesh sang the song. Later, Aadesh used Rosalie Nicholson's voice for the English parts used in the back drop.

After the box office success of the film, Aadesh asked Prakash Jha about this experiment.

'The story of my film was a modern-day adaptation of an old story. Naturally, I thought that fusing classical lyrics with modern composition might work best,' Prakash Jha replied.

A lot of time had passed since the release of the film. One day, I went to a dance club. While watching the youth dancing on the lines *'Mora piya mose bolat nahi, dwaar jiya ke kholat nahi'*, I was reminded of Prakash Jha who wanted to turn these classical sounding lines into a youth number. I once again applauded his vision and clarity it.

Movie: *Rajneeti* | Lyrics: Sameer | Singer: Aadesh Shrivastava | Music Aadesh Shrivastava

41

'Char Baj Gaye Lekin Party Abhi Baaki Hai'

2011

'Char Baj Gaye Lekin Party Abhi Baaki Hai' is one of those songs whose journey was extremely difficult, yet the result was extremely rewarding.

Noted choreographer Remo D'Souza was stepping into a director's shoes with *F.A.L.T.U.* (2011), and my opinion was sought on the choice of the film's music director. Being an urban, youth-centric film, I suggested the name of a young music director duo, Sachin–Jigar, whose work I had heard in the past and considered it to be much in accordance with today's times.

A meeting was arranged with Remo and the producer of the film, Vashu Bhagnani, whose son, Jacky was the hero of the movie. Remo informed them that the movie was heavily dance-centric, and so, the music was also to be in accordance with the same.

One by one, the songs of the movie were being written, until one day, I got a call from Sachin and Jigar. They were sounding excited, and on probing further, they informed me that they had come up with a tune that would be a sure shot blockbuster. Generally, when a music director comes up with a winning tune, the life of a lyricist becomes relatively easier. But over here, things were about to change.

The duo requested me to come up with a catch phrase that would appeal to the youngsters and be an instant hit. That set me thinking. There were several lines that came to my mind but none that really excited me. The only word that had stuck with me till then was 'party'.

Strange as it may sound, I remembered having seen the blockbuster hit *Om Shanti Om* (2007) where Bollywood superstar Shah Rukh Khan mouthed the famous dialogue '*Picture abhi baaki hai mere dost*'. For some reason, on remembering these lines at this time, I felt an instant connect. I felt that, when merged with our song, it would work wonders.

However, the phrase was still incomplete and needed closure. The best way to connect with the audience is, I believe, by putting forth their issues, problems or circumstances out in an engaging and entertaining manner. It was only a month back when a close friend of mine had come to my house and seemed perturbed. Noticing this aberration in his usual jolly mood, I asked him the reason for his worry. It virtually seemed as if he was waiting for me to ask this question. And the moment I did, he blurted out, 'Sameer Bhai, I am very worried for my son's future. He should be concentrating on studies but all he does is partying. *Kal toh subah ke char baje ke baad ghar lauta* (Yesterday, he came back home at four in the morning).'

How we sorted out his issue successfully is a tale for a different day, but this line set me thinking. What if I added the time to the party? It would be a line appreciated by both parents and the youngsters, albeit in different ways.

And that gave birth to the line '*char baj gaye lekin party abhi baaki hai*'. Needless to say, everyone from the creative team loved the line, and when sung alongside the tune created, it sounded even better. But there was still one problem that remained—that of the singer. Several names were suggested—from Sunidhi Chauhan and Shreya Ghoshal to other singers—who were actually called to record the audio. Sadly, it was not working the way we had envisaged it.

As we all sat down to deliberate, one thing that I felt sure of was that the song had a very strong Punjabi undercurrent to it. This is why I suggested we get a singer who could do justice to both, the Punjabiness of the song as well as the rap the song contained. Unanimously, we all zeroed in upon Hard Kaur. Not only did she hail from Punjab but her ability to successfully rap had come to the fore in her hugely successful breakthrough song 'Ek Glassy'.

On hearing the tune, she was super excited and worked day and night to give it her best shot. And before we knew it, the song was done. Everyone, especially Jacky, was very happy with the soundtrack. But his father wasn't.

I remember Vashu ji initially being apprehensive of the song. It was, after all, his son's movie. It was but natural for him, both as an efficient producer and a loving father, that all went well. I went up to him and tried to assauge his fears. I told him to let the music get released and that it would be a big hit.

What happened thereafter is for everyone to see. Not only did the film become a hit at the box office, the song became a chartbuster. Even to this day, whenever I perform this song at various concerts of mine, the crowd and especially the youth go ballistic, irrespective of whether it is past 4.00 a.m. or not!

Movie: *F.A.L.T.U.* | Lyrics: Sameer |
Singer: Hard Kaur | Music: Sachin-Jigar

42

'Saibo'

2011

Friends, let's talk about 'Saibo', the sensational hit song of Tusshar Kapoor starrer 2011 film *Shor in the City* (2011). The film was produced by Ekta Kapoor and directed by duo Krishna D.K. and Raj Nidimoru. Not only 'Saibo', all the songs of the film were very good, but my experience of this film turned out to be the worst of my career.

This was my third and final film with music director duo Sachin–Jigar. My meeting with them used to happen sometimes at Rajesh Roshan's office and sometimes at Pritam's office. Jigar used to assist Rajesh Roshan, and Sachin used to work with Pritam. After some time, both of them started working as a team. Before working in Hindi cinema, both of them had composed background music and songs for TV serials, Gujarati plays and ad-film jingles, and had a good knowledge of Gujarati folk music. Both used to meet me very humbly and often used to say, 'Sir, please introduce us to any film producer as independent music directors.'

'Show me some of your work, then I will see what I can do for you guys.' This used to be my response to them.

Frankly, I too was looking for an opportunity to work with composers from young generation because it is the only way you can judge yourself regarding how fresh your thinking is. This also keeps you updated and aligned with the times.

Sachin–Jigar composed some songs and presented them to me, which I really liked and appreciated. I genuinely felt that they were a talented duo, and that if they got a push, they could go much further. Keeping this in mind, I introduced both of them to my old friend and the famous film director Satish Kaushik. Satish also liked their work and signed them on for his next, titled *Tere Sang* (2009). Although the film didn't do well, Sachin–Jigar's work was appreciated. Next, we worked together in Vashu Bhagnani's film *F.A.L.T.U.* (2011). The soundtrack of *F.A.L.T.U.* was a big hit, and our work was highly appreciated. The song 'Char Baj Gaye' was a gratifying discotheque experience for party animals. It was simply a chartbuster!

After *F.A.L.T.U.*, here we were again together to work in Ekta Kapoor's *Shor in the City*. The three of us were overjoyed to see the possibility of composing great music in the film, and we started working on the album with great enthusiasm.

One day, both of them came to me with a suggestion.

'Sir, in Gujarati folk, there is a word "saibo". We can make a good song using this word.'

Since they had a good understandig of Gujarati folk music, I liked their suggestion, and we started working on the song using 'saibo' as the hook.

Both of them then started working on the composition and came up with an amazing tune, over which I wrote the lyrics. Shreya Ghoshal and Tochi Raina were called on to dub the song. Shreya's mesmerizing voice led 'Saibo' from romanticism to perfection, whereas Tochi's peculiar singing gave the song the feeling of a blooming love-chemistry. Everyone on the team was very confident about the success of the song. Once the music was released, people loved all the songs, but 'Saibo' turned out to be the most loved song of the album and one of the most successful numbers of that year. The song is still fresh in people's memories.

Before the music release, everything was fine but I was surprised when I saw one more name along with mine for writing the additional lyrics to 'Saibo'. My credit for writing the lyrics was co-shared with a Priya Panchal. At that time, she was Jigar's girlfriend, and later they got married. I'd often seen Priya at the music sittings and recordings with Sachin–Jigar. Something like this had never happened to me in my entire career. I was very angry, and therefore I called Sachin–Jigar for clarification.

'Why did you guys do this to me?' I wanted to hear an explanation from them.

Instead of confronting my anger, they surrendered and gave a very silly excuse.

'Sir, I'm going to marry her and couldn't refuse her the credit,' Jigar replied to me apologetically.

'But how can you add some lines in my song without my permission,' I asked Jigar, still irate.

'Sir, she'd written a few folk lines that we liked so we used them in the song,' Jigar gave me a very unprofessional excuse.

'You know, I can drag you to court for this breach of trust,' I yelled in anger.

They feared that I would take legal action against them, so they started requesting me to be kind with them.

'Sir, our career will be finished if you take us to court,' they pleaded.

Before getting the film, they had promised to work with me for five years, and we had even signed a contract for the same. I went inside my house to get the contract and tore it into pieces right in front of them.

'I always believed in my talent, not in any piece of paper. Since I now know your intentions, it is impossible for me to work with you. You guys are free to work with whosoever you want.' These were my last words with them, and we haven't spoken since.

Even today, when I hear this song, those events come back running to my mind. However, I will always remember both, the sweet memories and the bitter experience of this film. But fortunately, this experience has not made me so bitter that I should be wary of the younger generation and break my ties with the young talent of Bollywood.

I have great hope from the youth of this country, and I will always look forward to working with them. Most recently, I was really overwhelmed seeing outstanding work of some really young musicians in Bollywood. I pray for their health and success because they are our future. And I hope that, along with great talent, they will also bring great professionalism to our industry.

Movie: *Shor in the City* | Lyrics: Sameer | Singers: Shreya Ghoshal, Tochi Raina | Music: Sachin–Jigar

∽

43

'Balma'

2012

I know Himesh Reshammiya as a hard-working music director who is blessed with god-gifted talent and a great sense of music. I consider the movie *Khiladi 786*'s (2012) music album extraordinary and among Himesh's best work.

Since Himesh was not only the music director and actor in this film but had also donned the cap of the producer, there was even more responsibility on his shoulder. He, therefore, wanted to experiment with the music and come up with something fresh. This film marked Akshay Kumar's return to the *Khiladi* film franchise after 12 years. All the songs had been composed, but we were stuck at one song. Himesh wanted to surprise Akshay Kumar with a mind-blowing composition for him to dance on.

'Sir, I'm big fan of R.D. Burman and want to dedicate a song to his musical genius,' Himesh opened his heart and said to me.

'What do you have in mind?' I asked Himesh wanting to know more.

He didn't say anything that day, instead he asked me for some money to get back home.

One day, he called me to his studio and presented to

me a music track. The composition was foot-tapping and instantaneously engaging. I was hooked to the track on the spot.

'Sameer ji, write the best song of my career,' Himesh smiled and said to me.

I started working on the track and wrote something. But one day, Himesh called and demanded that I bring the words 'fire brigade' into the song. I laughed at his demand.

'What are you saying Himesh?' I replied to him in disbelief.

'Sir, why don't you just try. I'm sure, it will come,' Himesh replied, adamant like a child who absolutely couldn't live without a toy of his choice.

He took me through the idea of the dance number once again. As per him, the girl in the song was young and beautiful. She had a fire within and needed to extinguish that fire. That is how Himesh wanted to bring in the fire brigade into the song.

'I got it, brother. But what will I do with the *qaafia* and radeef?' I was referring to the rhyming pattern of the words 'fire brigade'.

'You will figure it out, sir!' He hung up the phone leaving me with a poetic challenge.

I have always loved challenges. It wasn't a routine romantic song. It was a conceptual item song. After few days of trials and errors, I was finally blessed with the second line of the song: *'Tera rasta dekh rahi hoon, sigdi pe dil sek rahi hoon, aa pardesi more balmaaaa... Oh balma...'*

Now, it was very easy for me to write the first line of the song: *'Fire brigade mangwa de tu, angaro par hain armaan... Oh balma...'*

When I met Himesh with the mukhda, he got emotional and hugged me tightly.

'Sir, now I can proudly dedicate this to Pancham Da. It's

a totally mind-blowing song,' Himesh complimented me.

After the desired mukhda, the challenge was to complete the song. We sat together for a couple of music sessions and completed the song, which we were sure was going to become the chartbuster of the year.

Akshay Kumar, Asin and the Polish-German model Claudia Ciesla loved the song 'Balma'. It was a retro foot-tapping item number, which was wonderfully sung by Sriram Chandra. Shreya Ghoshal's husky voice had added the desired oomph to the song. The song was a tribute to the late R.D. Burman, or Pancham Da as he was fondly referred to, whose presence can be experienced not only in the video but also in the composition, which is inspired by his blockbuster number 'Mehbooba Mehbooba' from *Sholey* (1975). Himesh instructed both his singers to bring in the passion and the sound of the mesmerizing song.

The song was shot brilliantly in which Akshay was shown romancing Claudia and Asin, who he reunited with after their last big screen hit *Housefull 2* (2012).

The catchy lyrics and peppy composition of 'Balma' made it the sensation of the year. We knew that it was a hit song but never thought that it would be so massive. Whoever heard the song just loved it in totality.

I think you cannot always offer the same thing to the listeners again and again. People also get bored of hearing one type of sound repeatedly. They're always looking for new voices, new compositions, instruments and lyrics. According to me, people loved 'Balma' because it was an absolutely new sound to the listeners.

Today whenever I hear this song, I really like the groove and the tempo, along with Akshay's energy and that of the dancers, who wonderfully added the 'fire' through their performance. Reaching on the level of Pancham Da was always challenging and never easy. We had successfully made a song which sounded like arguably his most memorable number. Yet it was a different sound for the listeners. It was a super hit package for the audience.

Whenever Himesh's hit songs with me will be counted, the discussion will not be complete without the mention of this song because this is one of the best songs of our career.

Movie: *Khiladi 786* | Lyrics: Sameer | Singers: Sreerama Chandra, Shreya Ghoshal | Music: Himesh Reshammiya

∽

44

'Daghabaaz Re'

2012

Superstar Salman Khan and Sonakshi Sinha starrer film *Dabangg* was released in 2010 and had created magic at the box office. The music of the film was super hit too. Therefore, with everyone waiting for another 'Tere Mast Mast Do Nain', expectations were running high for *Dabangg 2* (2012).

I was contacted by the makers to pen the lyrics in the much awaited sequel of *Dabangg* and was asked to contribute with a bigger song than 'Tere Mast Mast Do Nain'. Initially, I had no idea what to write, but I took the job as a challenge. '*Tere mast mast do nain*' became a guiding line for me to move ahead because I wanted to come up with similar keywords in the new song. Since the film was set in North India, I started thinking around words like '*nain*', '*naina*', '*ankhiyan*', etc., which were spoken in Uttar Pradesh, but nothing was working out.

In the process of writing and deleting, I recalled a phrase '*daghabaaz re*' from an old song, which I was hooked to. To me, it was a very musical and romantic expression. The realization that this was the keyword that I had been looking for made me very happy. When I used it with the word 'naina', it sounded even more beautiful and soulful—'naina daghabaaz re'. But I was still not satisfied with the line. Something still felt amiss in the song. One fine morning, I added '*tere*' to it and immediately felt satisfied with how the complete line of the mukhda sounded—'*tere naina bade daghabaz re*'.

Next, my challenge was how to take the first line further. Finally, God almighty blessed me with a line '*Kal mile, hamka bhool gaye aaj re*'. Generally, poetry that we mostly hear refers to a lover complaining to his lady love that she has forgotten him. But here I could bring in the idea where, instead of complaining to a lover, the lover is talking to her eyes and complaining that they've forgotten him.

When I presented the lyrics to Sajid–Wajid, they were thrilled!

'This romantic number would be true to the spirit of "Tere Mast Mast Do Nain"!' Sajid said.

'We will bring the old Indian melody to this song,' Wajid said confidently.

'Salman Bhai's fans will go crazy over this for sure,' I replied enthusiastically.

Both the composers started working on the song with great excitement. Since *Dabangg* was an earthy and rooted film, it didn't require any peppy or modern numbers. Although, it did need a soothing Indian melody.

The treatment the composers gave to the song was very simple yet very engaging, pleasing and romantic. I loved the tune when I heard it for the first time. It took me straight to the golden era of Indian music and reminded me of the everlasting music given to us by Naushad, Shankar–Jaikishan, Mohammad Rafi Sahab and Lata ji.

Now, we had to take the song for dubbing. Since *Dabangg*'s 'Tere Mast Mast Do Nain' was sung by Rahat Fateh Ali Khan, therefore we decided to go with him this time as well. I always make sure to be present in the studio at the time of the dubbing of the song because I'm very particular about the pronunciation and sound of the words I write. But due to some engagement, I couldn't go to Dubai for dubbing this song. Sajid–Wajid assured me that since Rahat Sahab was a knowledgeable man and understood poetry, there was no need for me to worry about his diction. While dubbing the song in Dubai, Rahat Fateh Ali Khan got stuck at a point and asked Sajid–Wajid to call me to verify a particular word.

'Sameer Sahab, what does "*paraan*" mean?' asked Rahat Sahab.

'Bhaijaan, it means life. It is derived from the Hindi word "*pran*". In Bhojpuri, we call it "paraan",' I replied back.

'Oh, I got it, Sameer Sahab,' he said.

I could sense that he was relieved after talking to me.

It was a casual telephonic conversation, but when I heard the song, the modulation Rahat Ali Khan gave to the word 'paraan' was mind blowing. I immediately called to thank and congratulate him.

'Bhaijaan, I'm very pleased the way you sang, "paraan re",' I said.

'Sameer Sahab, I was not able to give a proper vocal expression till the time you told me the correct meaning of the word,' Rahat said.

I was really impressed by the professionalism of this celebrated singer. He comes from Pakistan and speaks Urdu and Punjabi, but the way he sang a Bhojpuri phrase 'paraan re', I'm sure not many from the current lot of singers of Hindi cinema could've sung it like that. It seemed like he was from the Bhojpuri belt and understood the regional language. He could've sung it without talking to me, but it is the commitment and dedication towards his work that makes him such a great singer.

After signing the film, it had been quite a challenge for

me to come up with a bigger song than 'Tere Mast Mast Do Nain'. And it gave me immense pleasure and satisfaction to know that the assignment had been accomplished and the goal achieved with a great outcome.

Rahat Fateh Ali Khan added a certain Sufi touch with his soulful voice, while Shreya Ghoshal mesmerized movie-goers with her melodious voice. That's how we created 'Daghabaaz Re', which became one of the chartbuster songs of 2012.

The objective through this book is to tell the listeners that the song they hear in five minutes comes to them after crossing many hurdles. That it is the contribution of many people, and not just one person. I give full credit to Sajid–Wajid for composing it so beautifully, and to Rahat and Shreya for rendering their voices and making it a mesmerizing number.

And last but not the least, I must mention superstars Salman Khan and Sonakshi Sinha for performing this song so convincingly on screen that their romance oozed out of the screens. The efforts of all these people made 'Daghabaaz Re' a memorable song

I often say that a great team makes a great product, and that one should not walk away with all the credit of its successes. 'Daghabaaz Re' was a perfect example of this thought.

Movie: *Dabangg 2* | Lyrics: Sameer Singers: | Rahat Fateh Ali Khan, Shreya Ghoshal | Music: Sajid–Wajid

45

'Anarkali Disco Chali'

2012

We in Bollywood are often driven by herd mentality. If a new actor or actress is launched and becomes successful, then every filmmaker starts hunting for similar faces. After a hit film, the entire film industry gets busy in making the same kind of movies or the search for the same subject starts. In similar fashion, if a song becomes a hit, then that successful song becomes a reference point and everybody gets busy making the same kind of song.

In the year 2010, Salman Khan starrer *Dabangg*'s super hit song 'Munni Badnaam Hui' was no different and had done the same for Bollywood. Every composer was asked to come up with a tune similar to the Munni song. In that rat race, hundreds of songs flopped miserably, while some left their imprint on the hearts of people. 'Anarkali Disco Chali' from the film *Houseful 2* (2012) is an item song that was one of the fortunate few that broke the charts.

After the super success of *Housefull* (2010), the producer of the film, Sajid Nadiadwala had announced *Housefull 2*. The film had already created a buzz among the audience. Along with Sajid–Wajid, I was called by the producer and the director, Sajid Nadiadwala and Sajid Khan. After a while, in the meeting, something which I had dreaded so often happened with us. Director Sajid Khan asked us to make a bigger song than 'Munni Badnaam Hui'. Sajid–Wajid and I looked at each other and, smilingly, nodded with a yes.

Coming back to the music room, the three of us were immersed in thought. *What could have been the hook word of the item song*. We were looking for such a word with a romantic connection. Just then, the word 'Anarkali' came to my mind, which was synonymous with love and romance. Anarkali immediately found a place in Sajid–Wajid's heart.

'Sir, it's very good! Now think around "Anarkali" and make a nice mukhda,' Sajid told me.

In the beginning, I wrote, '*Sare laundon mein mach gayee khalabalee, Anarkali disco chali.*'

We did a little work on it and presented it to Sajid Khan and Sajid Nadiadwala, which they liked at first. But later, Sajid Khan said, 'I love "Anarkali", and this is the final hook word for me. But I don't like "*sare laundon* (all the boys)". It sounds very general, even though it should be very specific.'

I also felt that Sajid was right, but writing a new mukhda was a big challenge for me. Even after 10–12 music sessions, nothing good was coming to my mind. All three of us were quite frustrated. We were clearly told that the song won't be recorded if it did not sound personal. We even thought of dropping this song.

'Sir, it is very difficult to create a new song altogether. And here we are halfway through, as we already have a hook word. We just need to find the correct words around it,' Sajid said to me.

Then I thought that just as Laila and Majnu, Shirin and Farhad, Romeo and Juliet, we do call Salim and Anarkali in same way, two names in one breath. I felt that just as Anarkali and Salim's romance was shown in the movie *Mughal-e-Azam* (1960), I should write the very same for this modern-day

Anarkali. Now I could see clearly what to write; it was just about knowing how to put the words in order.

'*Chod-chaad ke apne Salim ki gali, Anarkali disco chali*,' I wrote.

Everyone loved the mukhda and it was now locked in. But the struggles were yet not over. As I remember, keeping in mind what had happened to Anarkali in *Mughal-e-Azam*, I wrote that the Anarkali of today was not ready to be buried into a wall in the name of love, that instead she would leave Salim's world or any other place where her love is not respected.

The song was now completed and had come out really well, but there were many more hurdles in making this item song, and the next one was a little technical.

Sandeep Shirodkar was programming all the songs of this film. The rhythm he had created had a distinct Indian classical tone. In the process of changing it to a modern dance number, the rhythm was changed several times. Once the rhythm was set in place, we loved the groove he had made and the track was approved.

I have experienced this a number of times: if a song gets stuck in the beginning, it keeps giving you trouble till the end. So, the next challenge was deciding who should we call to sing it.

Many names were discussed, but in the end everyone agreed that Sunidhi Chauhan was a good choice. I was surprised how well Sunidhi sang the song, but when producer Sajid Nadiadwala heard it, he didn't like her singing style at all. He was sure that someone else should be dubbed instead of Sunidhi Chauhan. Finally Mamta Sharma, of 'Munni Badnaam' fame, was called on to sing the song. She too sang it amazingly well. Everyone loved and approved her voice and singing style. Except me.

Now, the next challenge was whom to call to sing the male part of the song. Since Mamta had sung it on a very high note, technically, the male singer would have to sing it on the double key note of the *sargam*. Only then the voices of the female and male singer could be balanced against each other.

We called many singers, but no one could sing on that high a note. Finally, Sukhwinder Singh was called because he is known for his high-note singing. Sukhwinder came and heard the song. But he said that he would not even try because he was afraid that he would damage his throat. However, since he had liked the song so much, before leaving the studio he made Sajid–Wajid an offer based on a condition. He told them that if the composers wanted him to sing this song, he would give it a try, but he would only do one take. If it worked out, then well and good, otherwise they would have to get someone else to do the song.

Sajid–Wajid agreed. Sukhwinder first memorized the song, then went to the mic and sang the entire song in one take. It was really amazing to see him singing. Everyone was very happy because now the song was ready.

Director Sajid Khan shot the song on Akshay Kumar, Mithun Chakraborty and other actors, but Malaika Arora set the screen on fire with her performance. The song became a sleeper hit on its release. Everyone loved Mamta Sharma's singing yet again. But if anyone were to ask my opinion, I would still prefer Sunidhi Chauhan's version which unfortunately couldn't see the light of day.

Movie: ***Housefull 2*** | Lyrics: **Sameer** | Singers: **Mamta Sharma, Sukhwinder Singh** | Music: **Sajid–Wajid**

46

'Chinta Ta Ta Chita Chita'

2012

When this song was first released, everybody kept tapping their hands on dining tables, school benches, office tables, even on each other's backs.

The song 'Chinta Ta Chita Chita' appeared in the 2012 movie *Rowdy Rathore*. The movie was an action drama directed by actor and choreographer Prabhu Deva. When this super hit song was released, everybody was confused, thinking what it means. Few thought that it is derived from Telugu, since the original film was in that language. Comedy shows in India made fun of it. According to them, the meaning of 'Chinta Ta Chita Chita' was that worry was similar to a funeral pyre. They meant that if we worried too much, we would end up dead. But, let me tell you that the words have no meaning, nor are they derived from Telugu. The song was made using few meaningless words. The words, '*chinta ta, chita chita*' were just used to get the words to rhyme to the music beats.

The song came to me as a challenge because director Prabhu Deva was not ready to drop the tune and wanted me to come up with new lyrics on the available composition. Each remake of this film had the same music with new lyrics. I was absolutely clueless initially about what to write on the clapping and the tapping.

Sajid–Wajid were a little reluctant about keeping someone else's tune in the film, so in place of this song, they recorded another song and presented it to the producers and the director. The song was appreciated by the producers. But Prabhu Deva was not interested in the song at all. After many unsuccessful music sittings, Sajid–Wajid knew that Prabhu Deva was not going to drop this tune. Finally, they approached me for giving that tune some words.

'Sameer ji, you can save us by writing new lyrics because Prabhu Deva can drop music directors but not this song,' said Sajid–Wajid.

'But what to write on this fast composition?' I responded.

'Sir, if we had any idea what to write on this composition then we would've written it ourselves,' they laughed helplessly.

I started reading on the character of Akshay Kumar who was playing a double role in the film. One was a fearless cop, and another was a petty thief from Mumbai, who falls in love with 'Paro' played by Sonakshi Sinha. Shiva sings this song after he sees Paro for the first time and immediately falls for her.

After watching the original film, I thought of taking the hand clapping moment from the film and I used it in the song by writing the following words that were going with Akshay Kumar's *khiladi* image. The lyrics I wrote were based on the image of Akshay Kumar. '*Duniya chale agadi, toh main chaloon pichadi*' was inspired by his image of trying different kind of cinema and roles. '*Main hoon bada khiladi*' was inspired from his *Khiladi* series films. '*Sumdi mein leke jaaon*' was inspired from his 'con lover' image from many films, such as *Hera Pheri* (2000) and *Heyy Babyy* (2007) I kept the mood of the song funny and little over the top throughout the song, which is the overall image of Akshay Kumar.

While writing the lyrics, I knew that this was something

new that I was attempting for the first time. I just tried to follow the metre of the composition and the sound of the original lyrics. When I presented the lyrics to Sajid–Wajid, they were blown away by it.

'Sameer ji, this is not just a song, you've written my complete biography,' said Akshay Kumar when he heard it for the first time.

'You've managed to create so many funny moments in the film while shooting the song,' I complimented Prabhu Deva.

'Sir, you gave me so many moments in the lyrics to play with. I'm thankful to you,' responded Prabhu Deva.

Prabhu Deva shot the song as an fun dance number. I contributed to the song with new lyrics. And finally, Akshay Kumar, Prabhu Deva, Kareena Kapoor, Sonakshi Sinha and south star Vijay added their on-screen magic to make it even bigger. On each creative level, the song was getting bigger and bigger.

The song 'Chinta Ta Ta Chita Chita' turned out to be the most popular song of the film with a high degree of entertainment value, where Akshay Kumar can be seen tapping his hands to the music. That itself has a certain comic effect. Even now, when some TV channel telecasts this song, hands and feet both begin to move.

Movie: *Rowdy Rathore* | Lyrics: Sameer | Singers: Mika Singh, Wajid Khan | Music: Sajid–Wajid | Original composition: M.M. Kreem

47

'Malang'

2013

Dhoom *3* (2013) was the third installment of the *Dhoom* series. It was an action thriller film written and directed by Vijay Krishnan Acharya and produced by Aditya Chopra. It featured Aamir Khan, Katrina Kaif, Abhishek Bachchan and Uday Chopra.

All *Dhoom* films have a special place in my career, and I'll always cheer the success of its songs. I still remember the moment when Aditya had called me for *Dhoom* (2004), the first of the series.

'Sir, you're a poet of super hit romantic songs. Now the world wants to see if you can write for an action film as well,' Aditya had challenged me.

I took the challenge boldly and wrote '*Dhoom machale, dhoom machale dhoom*,' which became a super hit song.

'Dhoom Machale' was a phenomenon created by not only me but the entire *Dhoom* team. After giving lyrics for so many successful Yash Raj Films, I was confident about getting calls from them for each project they announce, but my confidence was shattered when I read about the launch of *Dhoom 3*. I had been dropped from the team and finally *Dhoom 3* took off without me.

Days and months passed, and I kept following the media

reports related to the film. My favourite actor Aamir Khan was roped in for the latest film and I was missing the team, but nothing was in my control. I still remember, one of my industry friends called and asked me teasingly, '*Sir, kya dhoom machaye hue hain aajkal* (what is up these days)?'

I politely told him that I was not writing for *Dhoom 3*. I always thought that the *Dhoom* franchise was my right and it should've rightfully come to me, but I never complained to Aditya Chopra for being unfair to me. In due course, I got to know through a friend of mine that a couple of songs were written, composed and eventually dumped because Adi Chopra didn't like them.

One day, when I was busy in a music session, I missed Aditya Chopra's call. When I was done with it, I immediately called him back. 'Sir, are you upset?' said Aditya.

'Not at all,' I replied back warmly.

'Can we have a cup of tea together?' Aditya asked me.

I went to meet Aditya the next day. He received me affectionately as he always used to. Aditya looked a little concerned. He asked his secretary to not disturb us for some time.

'Sir, *Dhoom 3* needs you,' said Aditya, the most passionate director and producer of Bollywood.

'I was shocked to be dropped from the *Dhoom* team,' I registered my complaint, and I wanted to be upfront about it as well.

'*Dhoom* is your franchise and it will remain yours,' Aditya assured me, and then continued, 'I'm sorry for whatever happened. Sir, whenever I'm stuck, I think of you.' He looked apologetic while replying.

Aditya told me that two songs had already been dumped so far. He was not happy with the way the music of *Dhoom 3* was shaping up.

'Pritam is trying to convince me of a track which I don't like at all. Please have a look at it,' said Aditya, as we shook hands and ended the meeting.

I was so pleased to be back on board. I met Pritam the same day and heard the track that Adi had mentioned. Pritam sang dummy lyrics on the tune. Honestly, to me, there was nothing in the track that sounded odd.

'I like the track,' I said to Pritam.

'But Adi didn't like it. I've to make a different composition for him,' Pritam looked disappointed.

I assured him that the track is good and nothing more needs to be done with it. I suggested that maybe Aditya does not like his dummy lyrics, so we have to come up with fresh words on your tune. Pritam loved my suggestion and we started jamming and brainstorming. Meanwhile, Aditya had also joined us. I insisted him to narrate to me the story once again. I wanted to especially understand the character of Aamir Khan in the film.

Since Adi is a wonderful storyteller, he quickly took me through the script, which helped me understand the project a little deeper. The character of Aamir Khan in the film was very temperamental, moody and free-spirited.

After an hour-long music session, a word going well with Aamir's character came to my mind and I started singing the word '*malang malang*'.

Aditya jumped up in joy upon hearing the word on the tune. 'Sir, this is it. This is the keyword. Now you just have to dress it up,' said Aditya joyfully.

We ended the day in high spirits.

The word 'malang' has several meanings—it refers to a Sufi saint; it even means a mad man, a nomad or an easy-going person. So instead of giving it a romantic feel, I thought of giving a Sufi feel to the song, and that experiment of mine worked. After a few music sessions, I had completed the entire lyrics.

We presented the final song to Adi who loved and approved it in a single sitting. Pritam was very happy with the result. He thanked and hugged me warmly. I've had a great rapport with Pritam and most of our films together have been huge hits.

The song was rendered by Siddharth Mahadevan and Shilpa Rao wonderfully well. Vijay shot it brilliantly. Aamir Khan and Katrina Kaif performed it marvelously on screen, and both lived the characteristic of a malang.

If I think about the entire journey of *Dhoom 3*, I would like to humbly submit that I was overconfident in the beginning. I assumed that I'll be called to write the songs of the film and got disheartened when I was dropped from it. But all is well that ends well.

Movie: *Dhoom 3* | Lyrics: Sameer | Singers: Siddharth Mahadevan, Shilpa Rao | Music: Pritam

48

'Dard Dilon Ke'

2014

The Xposé, made under the banner of HR Musik, was a romantic thriller released in 2014. It was produced by Himesh Reshammiya and directed by Anant Mahadevan, and it starred Himesh and two gorgeous debutant actresses, Sonali Raut and Zoya Afroz.

When I see the life journey of Himesh, I cannot but be full of praises for him. He started his career by scoring background music for TV serials. From there, he went on to become one of the biggest music director of Hindi films. There was a time when his singing and his style of singing was being discussed everywhere. But soon after, he stepped into the world of acting and achieved the status of a successful actor by giving successful films one after the other. He remained a very fortunate person in every phase of his life.

One day, Himesh spoke his heart out to me, 'Sir, creating music for another star is different, while making it for myself is a different game. The pressure increases a lot. If the music doesn't work, then people will say "Himesh, you should've focussed on good music first." Therefore, for the films in which I am acting, I keep on working on the songs, making them better and better, until the very end.'

'I fully agree with you,' I replied.

The same happened with *The Xposé*. Himesh was very much concerned about every song of this film. His one habit that has always impressed me is his detailing. Whether it is his compositions, filmmaking, his acting, his singing, his wig style or his grooming and clothing, he gets immersed in everything, and that is the secret of his success. If you do any work with great dedication, success is certain.

'Sir, if you love me, then you've got to write a very passionate, romantic, and deep song for this film of mine as a token of love,' Himesh pleaded.

'Done, brother,' I replied back with a smile and a pat on his shoulders.

'I want young guys to listen to it again and again.'

Now his demands were increasing, I thought to myself. I laughed and nodded, happy to write for my favourite contemporary music director.

As per the promise, I now had to write a deep romantic song for him. But if we talk about romance, poets in each language have said everything there was to say, and there is nothing new left to be said. *What can I write that is new and deep*, I started wondering.

I was immersed in this thought when a couplet by the great Sufi poet Hazrat Amir Khusrau in Persian language passed through my mind. That's where my search ended. Khusrau had said:

Mun tu shudam tu mun shudi, mun tun shudam tu jaan shudi,
Taakas na guyad baad azeen, mun deegaram tu deegari.

This means:

I have become you, and you me, I am the body, you soul,
So that no one can say hereafter, that you are someone,
and me someone else.

I was sure that if I write about this idea in my song, then the youth of today will find this form of classy romance absolutely new and fresh.

I wrote, '*Dard dilon ke kam ho jate, main aur tu agar hum ho jate.*'

'It's awesome, sir,' said Himesh, full of excitement.

He loved this thought, immediately sat down to compose it and made a very soulful composition. I could see that this was also going to be another melodious song of his.

'I'll get Arijit Singh to sing this song,' said Himesh about the most popular singer of the time.

'Yes, his voice will definitely take this song to another level,' I agreed with Himesh's choice.

The track was ready, but Arijit was very busy doing concerts and recordings. The recording of this song was kept on hold and we waited the singer to give us the time to dub his voice. Director Anant Mahadevan planned the shoot in Paris. The date of the shooting was close by but the singer was still absent. We had to think about another singer because the shooting could not be postponed further.

'Why don't you sing it?' I suggested to Himesh.

'No sir, the song will not sound good in my voice,' he replied.

Seeing Himesh's professionalism and honesty, I was shocked that such a big singer himself was saying that this is not his song. Well, we searched for another singer, and then finally Himesh found a new singer in Mohammad Irfan. It was Himesh's greatness that he called Irfan to his HR Musik studio and told him the truth—that the first choice of this song wasn't him but Arjit Singh, and if he sang it well then everyone would forget that they had ever thought of someone else and not him. Himesh also gave Irfan confidence that if he sang the song well, then this song could become the turning point of his career.

'Sir, you called a new singer like me for such a big song, I will always be thankful to you for believing in me. Arijit Singh is a very big singer. I do not know whether I will be able to sing like him, but I promise you that I will give my best. Allah has always been kind and helpful to me,' Irfan spoke from his heart.

Irfan stayed true to his words and sang the song melodiously. When people heard it for the first time, they were confused whether it was sung by Arijit or by someone else. Irfan earned himself a lot of accolades with this song, and after that many more big songs came his way. We too were very happy with the track. Himesh went into further detailing around how this song would look great on the big screen.

'Dard Dilon Ke' was beautifully picturized on Himesh and Zoya Afroz at stunning locations in Paris. Himesh's performance as an actor was very impressive to me.

This song turned out to become one of the most popular songs of the season. The credit of the film's success also goes to its amazing album, and *The Xposé Returns* was announced thereafter.

Movie: *The Xposé* | Lyrics: Sameer |
Singer: Mohammad Irfan | Music: Himesh Reshammiya

49

'Tu Kheench Meri Photo'

2016

I've always enjoyed working with Himesh Reshammiya because he loves to experiment as a music director and serves something new to his audience each time. *Sanam Teri Qasam* (2016) is one such film that will be remembered for its super hit music. I'd earlier penned successful songs for duo Vinay Sapru and Radhika Rao in their directorial debut film *Lucky, No Time For Love* (2005). Before directing films, they'd earned a big name by directing memorable music videos. 'Yaad Piya Ki Aane Lagi' was one of their successful ventures. Therefore, their understanding of music and shooting the songs was really mind blowing.

When I was offered *Sanam Teri Qasam,* I laughed remembering *Aashiqui* (1990), a very important film of my career. After 16 years, the same kind of situation and challenge was again in front of us: the music team. *Aashiqui* had a new hero and a new heroine, and it did well at the box office because of its super hit music. Yet again, here was a romantic film with a new star cast. South star Harshvardhan Rane and Pakistani actress Mawra Hocane were getting launched with this production. If the lead pair in the film is fresh, then producers depend upon the music to be a hit, which can eventually pull the viewers to the box office. With such films, the pressure is more on the music team than on one with a big star cast. Finally, we took the challenge head on and started working to create music that was going to be remembered for long.

Himesh and I started our music sessions, which went on for a few months. Vinay and Radhika were adamant about recording all the songs before starting the shoot. So, we finished almost all the songs, but got stuck at one. Regarding the situation of the song, we were briefed that a young couple is on a trip and the girl is drunk and is singing the song. I was thinking what to write on this situation?

'Sir, can we do something around, "Selfie le le re" song?' Radhika suggested.

'Sameer ji, the word "selfie" has been done to death. Let's try something else,' Himesh was clear that he wasn't interested in the word 'selfie'.

Taking selfies had become a huge trend at that point in time. Right from Prime Minister Narendra Modi to Salman Khan, everybody was talking about selfies. Social media was flooded with selfies and there seemed to be no stopping it. Because Radhika's suggestion was brilliant to begin with, I took it as a challenge to represent the same idea in different words.

After a fortnight, Himesh was ready with his tune and it sounded absolutely brilliant. I was still in search of a keyword. Everybody loved the tune and they all were looking at me for the lyrics. I requested all of them for a little more patience and bought more time to think. At the end of the session, I gave my mobile phone to my driver to click a picture with Himesh, Radhika and Vinay.

'*Ek* photo *kheech lo hamari* (Please take a photo),' I asked my driver.

While he was clicking the photo, I smiled on recollecting what I'd just said to my driver.

'"*Kheech meri* photo" can be our hook-line,' I said to Himesh excitedly.

Everyone loved the hook-line, and instead of concluding the session, we all went inside the studio and re-started the session with great enthusiasm.

On the mic, Himesh sang the line, but it came a little short, so I added '*tu*' in the beginning and '*piya*' at the end of the line, and it came as perfect. Vinay and Radhika were brimming with happiness upon listening the hook of the tune!

'Sir, we got the song!' said Vinay cheerfully.

Finally, we had the mukhda of the song. Now I had to complete the lyrics, but it was easy since I knew what I had to write further, now that I had the mukhda with me. I completed the lyrics quickly after that. The song was wonderfully sung by very talented singers Darshan Raval, Akasa Singh and Neeti Mohan. It came out as a very youthful dance number. Yet again, the multi-talented Himesh proved why he was loved by the entire nation.

Vinay and Radhika treated the song as a crazy fun number. Although, it must have been very difficult for them to shoot it at a real railway station and a crowded market with newbie actors, Mawra Hocane and Harshvardhan Rane, how they managed to avoid any major mishaps is commendable! I was very proud to see our song receive the same amount of success as 'Selfie Le Le Re'. We'd taken the inspiration from 'selfie', yet this felt different.

The song became an overnight hit and undoubtedly a youth anthem. Girls were found playing this song and taking selfies. Although the film didn't do well at the box office, the production company must've recovered their money from this song alone.

Remembering the whole story, I just want to say that it is always very difficult to write something with inspiration from a successful song. Initially the fear I had was that I would mess the song up completely, or that I will end up writing the same thing. But those who try never fail.

If I had refused to listen to Radhika that day, then the world would never have heard this wonderful song. Here I would like to recollect a beautiful saying of a wise man, 'Do not pay attention to who is saying it, but at what is being said.'

I'm glad I had heard both Radhika and Himesh that day. Radhika inspired me for the song, and Himesh advised me not to use the overused word 'selfie'.

Movie: *Sanam Teri Qasam* | Lyrics: Sameer |
Singers: Neeti Mohan, Akasa Singh, Darshan Raval |
Music: Himesh Reshammiya

50

'Ek Chumma'

2019

I wrote the songs for *Housefull* (2010) and *Housefull 2* (2012), along with many other hits for film producer Sajid Nadiadwala. When he told me that he was planning to have more than one lyricist in *Housefull 3* (2016), I left the project saying that till date I had written only solo films for him, and I had never given him cause to complain—neither about the deadlines nor about the final product, which was almost always a super hit. I was therefore taken aback by his decision and simply told him to think about me when he planned to have just one lyricist for a film.

Time passed, *Housefull 3* released, and despite the promotion and the airplay, the songs from the film could not find a place in the hearts of people like the songs of the previous two films. Various formulae and experimentation were done to create memorable songs. I was shocked to know that the makers even tried four lyricists in one song. I can't imagine how four lyricists can be credited for one song. Due to all these experiments, the music of *Housefull 3* turned out to be the worst in the franchise.

It was time for *Housefull* 4 now, and Sajid remembered what I had said to him before. One day, he invited me to his office for tea.

'Baba, let bygones be bygones. Now, you have to give me a big song,' Sajid smiled at me in his friendly manner. He fondly calls me Baba.

Sajid then gave me a brief description of the fourth *Housefull* film and the songs. He also reminded me that I had promised him a hit song earlier sometime on the hook word '*chumma*', which I had promised to write for him after listening to the superhit song 'Jumme Ki Raat' from the Salman Khan starrer movie *Kick* (2014).

I immediately nodded and made up my mind to write a big 'chumma' song. Many songs, including Amitabh Bachchan's 'Jumma Chumma De De', were written on the same hook word and almost all of them became very famous, which is probably the reason behind Sajid choosing it. This was not difficult for me, as I had written many superhit item songs in the past like 'Sarkai Lo Khatiya Jada Lage', 'Chane Ke Khet Mein', 'Main Aayi Hoon UP Bihar Lootne', etc.

I was wondering what should I write that would be fresh and unique to listen to. The same evening, an old friend of mine called me and gave me the good news of his purchasing a new flat and invited me over to dinner at a five-star hotel to celebrate. I congratulated him and excused myself from the occasion saying that I was a bit busy. In response to my excuse, he immediately replied, '*Arre bhai! Aisi khushi par* dinner *to banta hai.* (A dinner is a must to celebrate this happy news)' That 'banta hai' phrase started echoing in my head and I felt that it is a phrase which is commonly used in ones daily life, and that is why it was relatable. After some brain storming, I was blessed with the lines:

Maine tujhe bachaya hai,
Gundon se chudwaya hai
Pooch le samne janta hai,
Ek chumma to banta hai.

After writing these lines, I felt that they were absolutely perfect and now nothing could be written to make it better. But when music director Sohail Sen and I went to narrate the mukhda to Sajid Nadiadwala, he loved the lines but said, 'Baba, before these lines, write something more, because this song is going to be shot on three heroes and three heroines, including super star Akshay Kumar. That's why I want to give a good buildup to this song first and then what you have written will come.'

This was unforeseen, but I readily took on the challenge. I was very confident. Sajid had placed these lines not in the beginning of the song, but made it the hook of the composition. I sat down, put my mind to it and thought that since the tune of the song was quite contemporary and the groove too was upbeat, I should be writing something modern as well. Finally I came up with:

Oh madam, Google wali,
Don't go, yon deke gali
Haan gundon se chhudaya hai,
Maine tujhe bachaya hai

And then I came on the earlier written line—'*ek chumma to banta hai*'. The lyrics were liked by everyone, so we locked it in. Now it was our turn to dub the song with a dummy voice so that we could present it to Sajid Nadiadwala for approval. We had started wondering about who could be brought on to sing this song, and just then a new singer dropped in at Sohail Sen's office looking to work with him. Seeing him, Sohail asked him to sing the dummy version. The boy was a very good singer, and his name was Altamash Faridi.

Hearing the dummy version, Sajid and everyone else loved it and it was immediately greenlit. From Mika Singh to newcomers, many big and small names were discussed for singing the song, but we could not decide on any particular singer. Finally, I suggested that why not listen to the voice of the new singer again. When we all heard the dummy version again, everyone felt that his voice sounded much better than all the established singers on this song. He was sounding new and fresh, which was also the energy Sajid was trying to bring with *Housefull 4*.

When Altamash was told that now he had been chosen as the lead singer, he became very emotional and could not believe his ears. Altamash and Jyotica Tangri sang the final version of the song with great enthusiasm.

Sajid Nadiadwala was very pleased with the final version and told us that he would make a grand video out of it. One day, after the shoot was over in the United Kingdom, he called me to a studio in Mumbai, 'Baba, come I want show you something magical.'

Sohail and I went to the studio. We were so thrilled to see the music video of the grand 'Ek Chumma' song. Choreographer Farah Khan had shot it amazingly well in London. With six big stars and thousands of dancers, the scale of the song was grand, and it was really looking much bigger and better than I had imagined it while writing it.

The song became an instant hit as soon as it was released. There would be hardly any person in the world who is a fan of Hindi cinema and has not heard this song. This song made singer Altamash Faridi a big star overnight.

Movie: *Housefull 4* | Lyrics: Sameer | Singers: Altamash Faridi, Sohail Sen, Jyotica Tangri | Music: Sohail Sen

Acknowledgements

I am overwhelmed with gratitude for the incredible individuals who have played pivotal roles in bringing the book *Lyrics by Sameer* to fruition.

First and foremost, I extend my deepest thanks to Shuja Ali, my esteemed co-author and accomplished film director. Your creative vision and storytelling prowess have enriched the narrative of this book. Our collaborative efforts have truly made this project a labour of love, and I am honoured to have shared this journey with you.

My heartfelt gratitude to our literary agent, Suhail Mathur, and the entire team at The Book Bakers for their support, guidance and dedication throughout this literary venture. Suhail, your belief in the power of words and music has been a driving force, and I am truly grateful for our collaboration.

My sincere appreciation goes to Rupa Publications for their trust in this project and for providing a platform to showcase the tales behind the lyrics. Their commitment to literature and music is commendable, and I am grateful for the opportunity to share my experiences through this esteemed publishing house.

To my guru, my father and my inspiration, the esteemed lyricist the late Anjaan, along with my mother, family members and friends, I express an earnest thanks. Their encouragement and support have been the foundation of my resilience. Their belief in my artistic abilities has fuelled my passion for poetry, and I feel truly fortunate to be embraced by such an extraordinary support network.

A special note of thanks to all my colleagues—especially Nadeem–Shravan and the late Sawan Kumar ji—who joined me in creating some of the most melodious music during the vibrant era of the 1990s and 2000s. Our collaborative efforts have left an indelible mark on the hearts of music enthusiasts, and I cherish the memories we have created together.

Last but certainly not least, I express my deepest gratitude to you, the reader, all my fans, and music enthusiasts and listeners. You have been a source of inspiration. Your love for lyrics and music motivates me to continue this artistic journey. I am humbled by the connection we share through the magic of melodies.

—Sameer Anjaan

∽

I express my sincere gratitude to Sameer Anjaan ji for endorsing and embracing the idea of creating a book centred on his songs. He proved to be an exceptionally cooperative co-author, displaying a commendable ease in collaboration. His consistent appreciation for everything I wrote added to the overall positive experience. What stood out was is his prompt responsiveness, making communication smooth and efficient. Despite being a celebrated figure, his humility and grounded nature have been a true testament to his character. I am grateful for the opportunity to contribute to this project alongside such a talented and humble individual.

I attribute my journey as an author to my dear friend Suhail Mathur and his literary agency The Book Bakers. Suhail's conviction, rooted in the belief that my extensive experience as a film director and screenwriter endowed me with the ability to craft a compelling book, instilled a profound sense of confidence in my authorial capabilities. I extend my heartfelt gratitude to Suhail Mathur and The Book Bakers for their steadfast guidance and support, and for their pivotal role in nurturing an emerging writer like myself.

I extend my sincere gratitude to the people at Rupa Publications, a distinguished Indian publishing house, for graciously accepting my book *Lyrics by Sameer*. Their encouragement and belief in a debutant author like myself, particularly in embracing a concept that holds deep personal significance, are truly appreciated. I would like to express my thanks to Rudra Narayan Sharma for his unwavering support throughout the publishing process.

From the depths of my heart, I convey profound gratitude to my wife, Shagufta Ali, and my children, Zainab Ali and Mohammad Abbas Ali, who have been steady pillars of support throughout my journey as an author. Their encouragement, confidence-boosting and genuine appreciation for the chapters I wrote played a pivotal role in shaping my path. They were the first to affirm that my writing was not only interesting but also engaging, making their support truly invaluable.

Special thanks go to my brothers, Sayed Asif Jah and Sayed Wasi Saeed, for standing by me through thick and thin and providing constant encouragement in whatever I do.

I extend heartfelt thanks to my mother, a perpetual source of inspiration, whose passion for writing poetry, short stories and travelogues profoundly influenced and motivated me to embark on this writing journey. Her unwavering commitment to the art of expression has been a guiding light. I also owe thanks to her and my father for imparting the education and instilling the values that formed the bedrock of my journey, shaping me into not only an author but also a better individual.

I am grateful to my late maternal uncle, Dr Rahi Masoom Raza, an accomplished screenwriter and author, whose influence enlightened my understanding of the respect and regard authors command in this world.

Finally, I wish to express my genuine gratitude to my family, friends and all my teachers. I acknowledge the love and support they have offered for this book and through life.

—Shuja Ali